yummy

yummy

desserts you can make in 5 to 30 minutes

CAROLINE BREWESTER

DUNCAN BAIRD PUBLISHERS

LONDON

yummy

Caroline Brewester

DEDICATION
For Dominic and Aurelia—you are both truly yummy.

ACKNOWLEDGEMENTS
Thank you to Dominic, Tutu and all of my friends who gleefully expanded their waistlines while tasting the recipes from this book and always asked for second helpings. Also a big thank you to Grace and Nicole for their hard work and unstinting belief in this project, to William, Bridget and Manisha for the gorgeous photographs and styling, and to Borra for her ongoing support.

Distributed in the USA and Canada by
Sterling Publishing Co., Inc.
387 Park Avenue South
New York, NY 10016-8810

This edition first published in the UK and USA in 2010 by
Duncan Baird Publishers Ltd
Sixth Floor, Castle House
75-76 Wells Street
London W1T 3QH

Managing Editor: Grace Cheetham
Editor: Nicole Bator
Managing Designer: Manisha Patel
Studio photography: William Lingwood
Photography Assistant: Isobel Wield
Food Stylist: Bridget Sargeson
Assistant Food Stylist: Jack Sargeson
Prop Stylist: Rachel Jukes

Library of Congress Cataloging-in-Publication Data

Brewester, Caroline.
  Yummy : desserts you can make in 5 to 30 minutes / Caroline Brewester.
     p. cm.
  Includes index.
  ISBN 978-1-84483-969-8
  1. Desserts. I. Title.

TX773.B756 2010
641.8'6--dc22

                                    2010018630

10 9 8 7 6 5 4 3 2 1

Typeset in Variable
Color reproduction by Bright Arts, Hong Kong
Printed in Singapore by Imago

Publisher's Note: While every care has been taken in compiling the recipes for this book, Duncan Baird Publishers, or any other persons who have been involved in working on this publication, cannot accept responsibility for any errors or omissions, inadvertent or not, that may be found in the recipes or text, nor for any problems that may arise as a result of preparing one of these recipes. If you are pregnant or breastfeeding or have any special dietary requirements or medical conditions, it is advisable to consult a medical professional before following any of the recipes contained in this book. Ill or elderly people, babies, young children and women who are pregnant or breastfeeding should avoid any recipes containing uncooked egg whites.

For information about custom editions, special sales, premium and corporate purchases, please contact Sterling Special Sales Department at 800-805-5489 or specialsales@sterlingpub.com

Notes on the recipes
Unless otherwise stated:
• All recipes serve 4
• Use large eggs
• Use ripe, medium fruit, and fresh herbs
• Use unsalted butter
• 1 tsp. = 5ml • 1 tbsp. = 15ml • 1 cup = 240ml

contents

introduction

Who doesn't love dessert? Nothing beats something sweet and yummy at the end of a meal; something that tantalizes the taste buds and creates delightful memories not just for you, the cook, but for the people you feed as well. With so many daily demands on our time, it's tempting to settle for something "easy" like a chocolate bar, ice cream, or a few store-bought cookies, but although these substitutes may be convenient, they just don't compare to the satisfaction of a homemade dessert. Creating something from scratch, with the occasional assistance of good-quality, ready-made ingredients, doesn't have to take a lot of time, either. As the carefully chosen recipes in this book show, it really is possible to produce delicious desserts, from pantry to plate, in 30 minutes or less. This book shows you how to brighten up mundane midweek meals with a lavish last course that can turn dinner into an extraordinary event. All you need are some basic ingredients and a few easy tricks—which I'm about to share with you.

One of the best starting points for quick desserts is fruit. Whether it's summer or winter, keeping an assortment of fruit on hand opens up a world of opportunity when you want to whip up a treat. Some of the quickest fruit-based desserts can also be the healthiest. Choose fruits that are in season. They will be at their peak of ripeness, sweetness, and fragrance and bursting with so much flavor, they'll need very little added sugar. If you have fruits that have begun to overripen, using them in a quick dessert can resurrect them—they'll need hardly any cooking to reach the point of perfect tenderness. Use leftover berries as decoration or puree them into a sauce to enhance any dessert with color, flavor, and texture.

Hot desserts are always slightly special, as the mere act of switching on the oven implies a sense of thoughtfulness and effort, even if the preparation is rapid. Chilled packs of pastry, ready rolled and ready to use, mean that pies and tarts become a reality in mere moments. Cooking crusts separately from fillings and then uniting them at the last minute can radically reduce baking times, or, easier still, you can serve the separate elements in a more modern, "deconstructed" style. For simple, speedy sponge puddings, all you have to do is whirl together some eggs, butter, sugar, and flour in a food processor to make a cake batter, add your favorite flavors, and then bake them in individual ramekins. As a special final touch, crown these creations with some custard or liqueur-laced whipped cream.

If unexpected guests pop by, or you just have a sudden urge to splurge, some of the most creative confections can be made from everyday cupboard standbys. Keep some nuts, dried fruit and candied citrus peel on hand, and you're off to a good start. Chocolate chips are great because they save you the time it takes to chop a bar of chocolate into small pieces for melting. Steep a few raisins in rum for a sophisticated, adult affair; toast a few flakes of coconut for a tropical twist; or go to town with a luxuriously layered, cherry-capped Knickerbocker Glory (see page 76). Sweet, sticky extras, such as honey, maple syrup, and dulce de leche, are perfect for drizzles and dips, or for rippling through cream and yogurt.

Shortbread cookies and lady fingers are pantry stars that you'll be happy to have on hand when the need for a quick dessert arises. They have a long shelf life and are great served alongside other desserts. Best of all, they really shine when towered with fruit and cream, or dipped, dunked, or drenched in liqueur and layered into a tiramisù or trifle. Crushed or crumbled, they make a crunchy base for creamy cheesecakes and other treats, too. Varying the flavors according to any fruits you may have around means that the options are almost limitless.

Another way to make spontaneous desserts easier to whip up is to keep a tub or two of ice cream in the freezer. A simple scoop is a perfect partner to pie, and everyone adores an ice cream sundae. Frozen berries are another frosty asset. They require no pre-preparation and can be elegantly enrobed in warm white chocolate sauce; whizzed to make an instant ice cream or sorbet; pureed and rippled into crème fraîche; or paired with pastry for pies, crumbles, and tarts.

No matter how much time you spend making a dessert, it should always look good—if it looks good then it will taste good! A few seconds spent adding a swirl of sauce, a sprinkling of fine sugar, or a hint of mint leaves will elevate your creation into something that looks special. For an instant touch of elegance, decorate your dessert with chocolate curls simply by dragging a vegetable peeler along the side of a chocolate bar. Even a simple smattering of cocoa powder or a light dusting of powdered sugar will give a dessert a more polished presentation—or indulge your inner child and let rip with a rainbow of sugar sprinkles scattered over the top.

There's never too little time to whip up the perfect dessert, no matter what the occasion. Life is short. Make dessert fast!

mango-coconut sundaes (see page 12)

CHAPTER ONE

5-minute desserts

Five minutes may seem like too little time to make anything, but most kitchens are stocked with a few basics that can go a long way. Ripe fruits, frozen berries, sweet jams, and cream, for example, can form the base of some super-fast desserts. Use an electric mixer to whip cream in a flash, then ripple it with sweet papaya puree and mango to make sensational Tropical Fools. For a restaurant-style dessert, try Iced Berries with Hot White Chocolate Sauce—simply match frozen berries with the easiest mixture of warm chocolate and cream and the ingredients will melt together in just a couple of minutes. When you want a warm dessert, cook up some Crisp Cinnamon Puffs for a real melt-in-the-mouth treat. These recipes prove there's no such thing as too little time for dessert.

mango-coconut sundaes

Puréed mango makes a super-fast sauce for ice cream and is a great way to transform mangos, even slightly overripe ones, into a delicious treat.

2 cups coconut or vanilla ice cream
1/4 cup unsweetened flaked
   coconut
1 large mango
juice of 1 lime, plus extra to taste

1 Remove the ice cream from the freezer and let stand at room temperature to soften slightly. Put the coconut in a dry skillet and toast over very low heat, stirring occasionally, 2 to 3 minutes until golden brown. Immediately transfer it to a plate, spread it out, and set aside.

2 Meanwhile, cut the mango away from the stone and use a spoon to scoop the flesh into a blender, discarding the skin. Add the lime juice and blend 1 minute until smooth. Add more lime juice to taste, if necessary.

3 Divide half of the ice cream into four sundae glasses or deep bowls and drizzle half of the mango puree over it. Divide the remaining ice cream into the glasses, then spoon the remaining sauce over it. Sprinkle with the coconut and serve immediately.

bubbly berries

This is a quick but indulgent way to serve summer raspberries. First you eat the fruit, then you can enjoy the fruit-infused fizz as an after-dinner drink.

juice of 1 1/2 small lemons
1/4 cup powdered sugar
2 cups raspberries
1 3/4 cups medium white or rosé
   sparkling wine, chilled
4 mint or basil sprigs, to decorate
crisp cookies, such as cantucci or
   thin butter cookies, to serve

1 Put the lemon juice and powdered sugar in a small bowl and stir until the sugar dissolves. Divide the raspberries into four tall glasses and spoon over the lemon syrup.

2 Add the wine and decorate with mint sprigs. Serve immediately with crisp cookies.

watermelon with mint sugar

Mint-flavored sugar adds a fresh note to watermelon, as well as a pleasing color contrast.

1 Cut the watermelon into 4 wedges, then remove and discard the rind and cut the flesh into large chunks. Arrange the watermelon on four plates and set aside.
2 Put the mint and granulated sugar in a small bowl and crush together, using the back of a spoon, 1 to 2 minutes until all the oils have been released from the mint. (You can also do this in a mini-chopper or using a mortar and pestle, or on a cutting board, using the flat side of a large knife.) Sprinkle the mint sugar over the watermelon and serve decorated with mint sprigs.

2lb. seedless watermelon
1 large handful of mint leaves, finely chopped
2 tbsp. granulated sugar
4 mint sprigs, to decorate

orange-honey salad with toasted almonds

Throughout the Mediterranean and Middle East, fragrant fruit salads, such as this one flavored with a hint of cardamom, are popular desserts.

1 Using a small serrated knife, cut the peel and pith away from the oranges and discard. Slice the oranges on a lipped plate to catch and reserve the juice that comes out during slicing. Arrange the slices on four plates and dust them with the cardamom. Transfer the reserved juice to small bowl.
2 Add the honey to the juice and mix well, then drizzle the mixture over the oranges. Sprinkle with the toasted almonds and serve decorated with mint sprigs.

4 large oranges
a large pinch of ground cardamom
2 tbsp. honey
2 tbsp. toasted slivered almonds
4 mint sprigs, to decorate

seared pear with dolcelatte

Serve this quick, sophisticated dessert as an alternative to a cheese course.

sunflower oil, for greasing
1 large firm pear, halved, cored, and cut into 12 thin slices
8oz. dolcelatte, or similar blue cheese, thinly sliced
2 tbsp. honey

1 Grease a ridged cast-iron griddle pan or heavy-bottomed skillet and heat it over high heat. Cook the pear slices 1–1$\frac{1}{2}$ minutes on each side until browned. Remove the slices from the griddle and arrange them on four plates.
2 Arrange the dolcelatte slices alongside the pears, drizzle with the honey, and serve warm.

▶ broiled peach melba

The classic combination of peach and raspberry is given a new twist here by quickly broiling the peaches. The warm fruit and cold ice cream and sauce make a gorgeous contrast.

2 cups vanilla ice cream
4 small peaches, halved and pitted
2 cups raspberries
2 tsp. powdered sugar, plus extra if needed
juice of $\frac{1}{2}$ lemon

1 Preheat the broiler to high. Remove the ice cream from the freezer and let stand at room temperature to soften slightly. Put the peach halves on a baking sheet, cut-sides up.
2 Broil 2 to 3 minutes until warmed through. Meanwhile, put the raspberries, powdered sugar, and lemon juice in a blender or food processor and blend until pureed. Taste and add more sugar, if necessary.
3 Transfer the broiled peaches to four plates and top each one with a scoop of ice cream. Top with the raspberry sauce and serve immediately.

▸ iced berries with hot white chocolate sauce

The creamy hot chocolate sauce in this recipe combines perfectly with frozen berries.

4 cups frozen mixed berries, such as blackberries, strawberries, and raspberries

HOT WHITE CHOCOLATE SAUCE
1/2 heaping cup white chocolate chips
1/2 cup heavy cream

1 Divide the berries into four heatproof glasses or bowls and let stand at room temperature while you make the sauce.
2 Put the chocolate chips and cream in a heatproof bowl and rest it over a pan of gently simmering water, making sure the bottom of the bowl does not touch the water. Heat, stirring occasionally, 2 to 3 minutes until well blended and the chocolate melts.
3 Transfer the sauce to a heatproof pitcher and serve immediately with the berries, allowing each guest to pour some of the hot sauce over the berries.

5-minute desserts

nectarines with maple cream

It's easy to transform basic ingredients like crème fraîche by accenting them with different flavors, such as the maple syrup used here.

1 cup crème fraîche
finely grated zest of 1 lemon
5 tbsp. maple syrup
4 nectarines or peaches, halved, pitted, and sliced
amaretti cookies, to serve

1 Put the crème fraîche, lemon zest, and 1 tablespoon of the maple syrup in a small bowl and stir well, then set aside.
2 Arrange the nectarines on four plates. Add a large dollop of the maple cream to each plate and drizzle with the remaining maple syrup. Serve with amaretti cookies.

hot strawberries romanov

Warming the strawberries brings out their flavor and sweetness.

juice of 2 large oranges
$1/4$ cup granulated sugar
5 tbsp. orange-flavored liqueur,
   such as Cointreau
1lb. (about 3 cups) strawberries,
   hulled and halved or quartered,
   if large
$1/2$ cup heavy cream
1 tsp. powdered sugar
mint leaves, to decorate

1 Put the orange juice, granulated sugar, and 4 tablespoons of the
   liqueur in a small saucepan. Bring to a boil, stirring constantly. Add
   the strawberries and boil 30 seconds, then set aside.
2 Put the cream and powdered sugar in a bowl and beat, using
   an electric mixer, until soft peaks form, then beat in the
   remaining liqueur.
3 Spoon the strawberries and sauce into four bowls and top with
   the whipped cream. Decorate with mint leaves and serve warm.

charoset

This crunchy fruit salad, made with apples, dried fruit, and nuts, is traditionally served for Jewish Passover meals, but it's delicious at any time of the year.

1 Put the apples, raisins, and walnuts in a large bowl and set aside. In a separate bowl, whisk together the red wine, honey, and cinnamon, if using, whisking until the honey dissolves.

2 Spoon the sauce over the fruit and nuts and toss well, making sure the apple is well coated to prevent discoloration. Divide into four bowls and serve topped with yogurt and drizzled with extra honey.

3 Granny Smith apples, quartered, cored, and diced
$2/3$ cup raisins
$3/4$ cup chopped walnuts
$1/4$ cup fruity red wine, such as Beaujolais
$1/4$ cup honey, plus extra to serve
a pinch of cinnamon (optional)
Greek yogurt or crème fraîche, to serve

citrus-flavored crème fraîche dip

Flavored crème fraîche is great with fresh fruit. Vary the items to dip according to your tastes and the season.

1 Put the crème fraîche, powdered sugar, citrus zests, and orange juice in a bowl and mix well. Spoon the dip into a large ramekin or bowl and put it in the center of a large serving plate or board.

2 Arrange the fruit and muffin pieces and the cookies on the plate around the dip. Decorate with mint and serve with wooden skewers or small forks that can be used to spear the fruit and muffin pieces and dunk them in the dip.

1 cup crème fraîche
1 tbsp. powdered sugar
finely grated zest of 1 small lime
finely grated zest of 1 small lemon
finely grated zest of $1/2$ small orange, plus 1 tbsp. juice
1 large peach, halved, pitted, and cut into bite-size pieces
8 strawberries, hulled and halved or quartered, if large
1 large apple, quartered, cored, and cut into bite-size slices
1 large chocolate muffin or similar, cut into bite-size pieces
8 ginger snaps
1 mint sprig, to decorate

fruity couscous

Couscous cooks quickly and can be sweetened with juice
and fruits to make a delicious and unusual dessert.

3/4 cup quick-cooking couscous
1 1/2 cups apple juice
8 soft dried apricots, coarsely
  chopped
1/2 cup golden raisins
2 tbsp. pine nuts
honey, to serve
plain yogurt, to serve

1 Put the couscous and apple juice in a saucepan and bring to a boil
   over medium heat, stirring occasionally. Add the apricots and
   golden raisins and boil 1 minute.
2 Remove the pan from the heat, cover, and let stand 3 minutes
   or until all of the liquid has been absorbed. Meanwhile, put the
   pine nuts in a dry skillet and cook over medium heat, stirring
   occasionally, 2 to 3 minutes until golden brown. Uncover the
   couscous and immediately stir the pine nuts in with a fork,
   fluffing up the couscous as you stir.
3 Spoon the mixture into four bowls or, for a prettier presentation,
   pack it into four 7-ounce ramekins or molds and turn them out
   onto plates. Serve drizzled with honey and topped with yogurt.

chocolate-dipped cape
▶ gooseberries

Exotic sharp-sweet cape gooseberries covered in dark chocolate
make an elegant dessert.

1/2 cup dark chocolate chips
1 tbsp. butter
20 cape gooseberries

1 Line a baking sheet that will fit in your freezer with baking
   parchment. Put the chocolate chips and butter in a heatproof
   bowl and rest it over a pan of gently simmering water, making
   sure the bottom of the bowl does not touch the water. Heat,
   stirring occasionally, 2 to 3 minutes until the chocolate and
   butter have melted. Remove the bowl from the heat.
2 Meanwhile, peel back the papery leaves of the cape gooseberries
   but do not remove them. Twist the leaves together just above
   the point where they join the fruit. Dip the cape gooseberries into
   the chocolate, lift them out, and allow any excess to drip back
   into the bowl, then put them on the baking sheet to set.
3 If the chocolate is too runny, freeze the cape gooseberries
   1 minute to help them set. Peel the cape gooseberries away from
   the parchment, arrange on a plate, and serve.

tropical fools

Soft tropical fruits are ideal for blending and pairing with cream to make rich, irresistible fools.

2 papayas, halved and seeded
juice of 1 small lime
2 tbsp. powdered sugar
1 cup heavy cream
1 small mango, peeled, pitted,
   and cut into bite-size cubes
shortbread cookies, to serve

1 Scoop the papaya flesh into a blender, add the lime juice and powdered sugar, and blend 1 to 2 minutes until smooth.
2 In a large bowl, beat the cream, using an electric mixer, until stiff peaks form, then fold in the papaya puree.
3 Spoon the fool into four glasses and spoon the mango cubes over them. Serve with shortbread cookies.

jewelled winter fruit salad

Tropical fruits, such as persimmon and pomegranate, create a stunningly attractive dessert when served together. Make sure to use only soft, ripe persimmons – hard, unripe ones have a bitter, tannic taste.

1 pomegranate
juice of 1 large clementine
1 tbsp. powdered sugar
2 large persimmons, halved
   and each half sliced into
   6 half-moons
4 mint sprigs, to decorate

1 Halve the pomegranate and, using a fork, remove the seeds onto a plate, then remove and discard any white pith. In a small bowl, mix together the clementine juice and powdered sugar, stirring until the sugar dissolves.
2 Arrange the persimmon slices on a plate and sprinkle the pomegranate seeds over them. Drizzle with the clementine syrup and serve decorated with mint sprigs.

lemon possets

Lemon posset is a delicious dessert made with lemons and cream. This version is ready in double-quick time.

1 In a small bowl, mix together the lemon curd, zest, and juice. In another bowl, beat the cream, using an electric mixer, until soft peaks form, then fold in the lemon mixture until just combined, being careful not to overmix.
2 Spoon the lemon posset into four glasses and decorate with lemon slices. Serve with crisp cookies, if desired.

1/4 cup lemon curd
finely grated zest of 1 lemon, plus 2 tbsp. lemon juice
1 1/4 cups heavy cream
thin lemon slices, to decorate
crisp cookies, such as thin butter cookies or vanilla wafers, (optional) to serve

▸ virtually instant raspberry sorbet

Frozen raspberries can be blended into such a fabulous sorbet, you'll never want to buy store-bought versions again.

1lb. frozen raspberries
   (about 3²/₃ cups)
¹/₂ cup granulated sugar
2 tsp. lemon juice
4 ready-made meringues, to serve

1 Put the raspberries and granulated sugar in a food processor and blend 1 minute or until coarsely chopped. Stop and scrape down the sides of the food processor bowl as necessary.
2 Add the lemon juice and 2 tablespoons water and blend another 1 to 2 minutes until smooth. You may need to stop and scrape down the sides of the bowl halfway through.
3 Immediately spoon the sorbet into four bowls or glasses and serve with meringues.

banana-raisin panini

Toasted banana sandwiches are brought into the realm of dessert with sweet-scented cinnamon-raisin bread.

8 small slices of cinnamon-raisin
   bread
2 small bananas, peeled and
   thinly sliced
2 tbsp. butter, softened
honey, to serve
whipped cream, to serve

1 Preheat a ridged, cast-iron griddle or skillet over high heat or preheat the broiler to high. Lay out 4 slices of the bread on a work surface and arrange the banana slices over them. Cover with the remaining slices of bread, then thinly butter both sides of each sandwich.
2 Put the sandwiches on the griddle and cook 1 minute on each side until lightly toasted. If broiling the sandwiches, broil 1 to 2 minutes on each side.
3 Cut the sandwiches in half diagonally and stack on four plates. Serve drizzled with honey and topped with whipped cream.

papaya with three-way lime

Papaya and lime bring out the best in each other in this refreshing, low-fat dessert.

1 Remove the sorbet from the freezer and let stand at room temperature to soften slightly. Peel the papaya quarters and cut them into thin slices or bite-size chunks.

2 Arrange the papaya slices on four plates, or spoon the chunks into four glasses or bowls, then sprinkle with the lime juice.

3 Cut the pared zest into thin, needle-like shards. Top each portion of papaya with 1 scoop of the sorbet and sprinkle with the zest. Decorate with mint leaves and serve immediately.

1 cup lime sorbet
2 papayas, halved lengthwise, seeded, and cut into quarters
juice and finely pared zest of 1 large lime
mint leaves, to decorate

cinnamon-glazed grapefruit

A quickly broiled cinnamon crust adds warmth and sweetness to simple grapefruit.

1 Preheat the broiler to high and line a baking sheet with foil. Trim away a small sliver of peel from the bottom of each grapefruit half so that the halves will rest flat when you put them on the baking sheet. Slip a small, serrated knife between the flesh and skin of the grapefruit halves and cut around to loosen the flesh from the skin slightly. Put the grapefruit on the baking sheet, cut-sides up.

2 In a small bowl, mix together the brown sugar and cinnamon, then sprinkle the mixture evenly over the grapefruit.

3 Broil 2 to 3 minutes until the sugar melts and is bubbling slightly. Serve hot with yogurt for spooning over.

2 large grapefruit, halved horizontally
1/4 cup packed light brown sugar
1 tsp. cinnamon
plain yogurt or whipped cream, to serve

ginger syllabub

Syllabub is a traditional English dessert made with cream and alcohol. The addition of fresh ginger gives this a modern twist.

1½in. piece ginger root, peeled and grated
2 tbsp. powdered sugar
6 tbsp. ginger wine, such as Stone's, or sweet sherry
1¼ cups heavy cream
2 pieces candied ginger, chopped
crisp cookies, such as thin butter cookies, to serve

1 Put the ginger, powdered sugar, and ginger wine in a bowl and stir until the sugar dissolves, then set aside.
2 In a large bowl, beat the cream, using an electric mixer, until soft peaks form, then beat in the ginger mixture, being careful not to overmix.
3 Spoon the syllabub into four glasses or bowls and sprinkle the candied ginger over the top. Serve with crisp cookies.

affogato all'amaretto with biscotti

Affogato—ice cream "drowned" in coffee—has to be one of Italy's best-loved fast desserts. Here it is enhanced with the almondy notes of amaretto and biscotti.

2 cups vanilla ice cream
6 biscotti cookies
¼ cup amaretto liqueur
¾ cup hot espresso-strength coffee
cocoa powder, to serve

1 Remove the ice cream from the freezer and let stand at room temperature to soften slightly. Meanwhile, put 2 of the biscotti in a small plastic bag and, using a rolling pin, crush them into crumbs then set aside. In a small bowl, mix together the amaretto and coffee.
2 Divide the ice cream into four bowls or wide coffee cups. Pour the hot coffee and liqueur mixture over the ice cream and sprinkle the biscotti crumbs over the top.
3 Dust with a little cocoa powder and serve immediately with the remaining biscotti.

coffee granita

Granita, a traditional Sicilian specialty, has bigger ice crystals than a sorbet. This delicious, ultra-quick version is made by blending ice cubes and coffee in a food processor.

1 Dissolve the coffee granules in 2 tablespoons boiling water and set aside. Put the cream in a bowl and beat, using an electric mixer, until soft peaks form, then set aside.

2 Put the ice cubes in a food processor and blend 1 minute, or until coarsely crushed. Add the granulated sugar and coffee and blend 1 to 2 minutes until crunchy granules form. You may need to stop and scrape down the sides of the bowl halfway through.

3 Spoon the granita into four glasses or coffee cups and top with the whipped cream. Dust each granita with cocoa powder and serve immediately.

4 tsp. instant coffee granules
1/2 cup heavy cream
5 cups ice cubes
1/2 cup granulated sugar
cocoa powder, to serve

coffee parfaits

For a quick dessert, these layered sundaes have plenty
of contrasting textures and intense flavors.

1 Remove the ice cream from the freezer and let stand at room
  temperature to soften slightly. Put the cream, powdered sugar,
  and vanilla extract in a bowl and beat, using an electric mixer, until
  soft peaks form.
2 Divide half of the ice cream and then most of the cookie crumbs
  into four glasses or deep bowls, then top with the remaining
  ice cream.
3 Drizzle with the liqueur, then sprinkle with most of the
  remaining cookie crumbs and top with the whipped cream.
  Decorate with the chocolate coffee beans and the rest of the
  cookie crumbs and serve immediately.

2 cups coffee ice cream
$1/2$ cup heavy cream
$1/2$ tsp. powdered sugar
$1/2$ tsp. vanilla extract
2 giant double chocolate chip
  cookies, crumbled
$1/4$ cup coffee-flavored liqueur,
  such as Kahlúa
12 chocolate coffee beans,
  or 2 tbsp. chopped dark
  chocolate, to decorate

caramel-pecan popcorn

Popping corn is fun and takes almost no time. Drizzling it with
dulce de leche or caramel sauce makes a sweet and sticky end
to a meal.

1 Line a baking sheet with baking parchment. Heat the oil in a large
  casserole or stockpot with a tight-fitting lid over high heat.
  Add the popcorn, cover, and cook, shaking the pan occasionally,
  2 minutes or until the popping sound stops.
2 Spread the popcorn out in a single layer on the baking sheet and
  let cool 1 minute. Meanwhile, put the dulce de leche and cream in
  a small bowl and mix well.
3 Drizzle the sauce over the popcorn and sprinkle with the pecans.
  Serve informally, allowing everyone to help themselves.

2 tbsp. sunflower oil
$1/2$ cup popcorn kernels
6 tbsp. dulce de leche or caramel
  sauce
3 tbsp. heavy cream
$1/2$ cup pecan halves, coarsely
  chopped

caramel creams

Dulce de leche is a wonderful ingredient to keep in the cupboard for making quick desserts. Here it's rippled with rich vanilla-accented mascarpone for a truly decadent treat.

1 cup heavy cream
1 cup mascarpone cheese
1 tsp. vanilla extract
1 tsp. powdered sugar
1/4 cup dulce de leche or caramel
  sauce, plus extra to serve

1 Put the cream in a large bowl and beat, using an electric mixer, until soft peaks form. In a separate bowl, beat the mascarpone, vanilla extract, and powdered sugar until smooth (no need to clean the beaters first). Stir in one-quarter of the whipped cream to loosen the mascarpone mixture, then fold in the remaining whipped cream until just combined.

2 Spoon the dulce de leche over the cream mixture and stir once or twice to ripple it through the cream, being careful not to overmix. Spoon the cream into four glasses or ramekins and serve drizzled with extra dulce de leche.

5

5-minute desserts

crisp cinnamon puffs

A very fast fritter, these delicious little puffs are bursting with spicy-sweet goodness.

2 cups canola oil, for
  deep-frying
1 tbsp. powdered sugar
1/4 tsp. cinnamon
1/2 sheet of ready-rolled puff
  pastry, about 41/2oz.
plain yogurt, to serve

1 Heat the oil in a large heavy-bottomed saucepan or deep-fat fryer until it reaches 350°F and preheat the oven to 150°F. Meanwhile, mix the powdered sugar and cinnamon together in a small bowl and set aside. Cut the pastry into 16 x 1$\frac{1}{2}$in. squares.

2 Working in batches to avoid overcrowding the pan, fry the pastry squares in the hot oil 1 minute on each side until puffed and golden brown. Remove from the oil, using a slotted spoon, drain on paper towel, and keep warm in the oven while you make the remaining puffs. Return the oil to the correct temperature before starting each batch.

3 Dust the puffs with the cinnamon sugar, then turn them over and dust again. Serve warm with yogurt for dipping.

cannoli cream pots

The ricotta cream filling used in traditional Italian cannoli is quick to make and can be served as a dessert on its own. If you have extra time, serve these in the Brandy Snap Baskets on page 83.

1 Put the chocolate chips in a heatproof bowl and rest it over a pan of gently simmering water, making sure the bottom of the bowl does not touch the water. Heat, stirring occasionally, 2 to 3 minutes until the chocolate melts. Remove the bowl from the heat.

2 Meanwhile, in a large bowl, beat the ricotta and cream, using an electric mixer, 1 minute until smooth. Beat in the vanilla extract, powdered sugar, and liqueur, if using, then stir in the citrus peel and orange zest.

3 Divide the ricotta mixture into four ramekins or small glasses. Spoon the melted chocolate over the top and sprinkle with the pistachios. Serve with crisp cookies, if desired.

$1/4$ cup dark chocolate chips
$1^1/_2$ cups ricotta cheese, drained
2 tbsp. heavy cream
1 tsp. vanilla extract
1 tbsp. powdered sugar
1 tbsp. orange-flavored liqueur, such as Cointreau (optional)
$1/_3$ cup chopped candied citrus peel
finely grated zest of 1 large orange
2 tbsp. shelled unsalted pistachios, coarsely chopped, to decorate
crisp cookies, such as brandy snaps (optional), to serve

yogurt & cassis ripple (see page 36)

CHAPTER TWO

10-minute desserts

Ten minutes gives you time for a little extra preparation and the chance to add pizzazz to your desserts. Melt some sugar, stir in some cream, and you have a gorgeous homemade toffee sauce to drizzle over bananas, meringues, and whipped cream for a delightful Banoffee Pavlova. When you want to really indulge in something special, go for Tipsy Ten-Minute Tiramisù— layers of rich mascarpone, Marsala-soused lady fingers, and chopped chocolate make this a knock-out dessert with adult flare. Or impress everyone with fruity Fast Berry Ice Cream, which comes together in a food processor in the blink of an eye. These and the other recipes here prove just how easy it is to turn quick desserts into something magical.

yogurt & cassis ripple

Crème de cassis elevates yogurt into a quick dessert and adds a gorgeous splash of color.

2/3 cup blackberry yogurt
3 tbsp. crème de cassis liqueur, plus extra to serve
1 cup heavy cream
1 tsp. vanilla extract
1 tsp. powdered sugar
1 cup Greek yogurt
1-2 squares of white chocolate, to serve
8 blackberries, to decorate
crisp cookies, such as thin butter cookies, (optional) to serve

1 Put the blackberry yogurt and crème de cassis in a large bowl and mix well, then set aside. Put the cream, vanilla extract, and powdered sugar in a separate bowl and beat, using an electric mixer, until soft peaks form, then fold in the Greek yogurt. Spoon this mixture over the blackberry yogurt and stir once or twice to ripple the two mixtures. Be careful not to overmix.

2 Spoon the ripple into four glasses or bowls. Drizzle a little extra crème de cassis into the glasses and grate the white chocolate over the top. Decorate with the blackberries and serve with crisp cookies, if desired.

strawberry shortbread stacks

Crisp shortbread cookies layered with cream and strawberries make an irresistible summer dessert.

8oz. (about 1 1/2 cups) small strawberries, hulled and halved or thickly sliced, plus 4 whole small strawberries, reserved, to decorate
2 tsp. powdered sugar, plus extra to serve
1 tbsp. brandy (optional)
1 cup heavy cream
1/4 tsp. vanilla extract
8 round, thin shortbread cookies

1 Put the strawberries, 1 teaspoon of the powdered sugar, and the brandy, if using, in a bowl. If omitting the brandy, add 1 tablespoon water. Toss together, then let stand 2 minutes.

2 Meanwhile, put the cream, vanilla extract, and remaining powdered sugar in a large bowl and beat, using an electric mixer, until soft peaks form. Drain the liquid from the strawberries into the whipped cream and fold together.

3 Put 1 cookie on each of four plates and top with half of the strawberries. Top with half of the whipped cream, then add the remaining strawberries. Cover with the remaining shortbread cookies and crown each stack with a spoonful of the cream. Serve decorated with the reserved strawberries and dusted with powdered sugar.

stuffed dates

This quick sweetmeat, flavored with ground almonds and
a hint of orange, is popular in Morocco.

1 Put the almonds and powdered sugar in a small bowl and stir well.
   Add the orange flower water a few drops at a time, stirring until
   the almonds and sugar hold together and form a somewhat dry
   paste. You may not need all of the liquid.
2 Divide the paste into 12 equal portions and roll them into small
   logs. Open out the dates and put one piece of the almond paste
   in the center of each one, where the pit was, then push the sides
   of the date together to enclose the paste. Arrange the dates on
   a serving plate and serve dusted with powdered sugar.

1/3 cup ground almonds
3 tbsp. powdered sugar, plus extra
   to serve
1 tsp. orange flower water
   or orange juice
12 pitted dates, split lengthwise

mango & melon with mojito syrup

Lime, mint, and rum syrup—the flavors in the popular mojito
cocktail—are used here to transform a fresh fruit salad into
an exotic treat.

1 To make the syrup, put the mint and powdered sugar in a small
   bowl and crush together, using the back of a spoon, 1 to 2
   minutes until the oils have been released from the mint. (You can
   also do this in a mini-chopper or using a mortar and pestle, or on
   a cutting board, using the flat side of a large knife.) Stir in the
   rum, lime juice, and 2 tablespoons water, then pour the mixture
   into a bowl, scraping out any mint that sticks to the bottom of
   the bowl. Add the mango and set aside.
2 Remove the rind from the melon quarters and cut the flesh into
   bite-size chunks, then add them to the syrup.
3 Gently toss the fruit and syrup together and spoon the mixture
   into four glasses or bowls. Serve decorated with mint sprigs.

mint leaves from 4 large mint
   sprigs, plus 4 mint sprigs
   for decoration
1/4 cup powdered sugar
2 tbsp. white rum
juice of 1 large lime
1 large mango, peeled, pitted, and
   chopped into bite-size pieces
1 green melon, such as galia,
   cut into quarters and seeded

10

10-minute desserts

◂ strawberry bruschetta

Bruschetta is usually served at the start of a meal and covered with savoury toppings, but this sweet twist is a great way to end a meal. A slightly stale loaf of bread is ideal for this recipe.

1 Preheat the broiler to high. Toast the bread on both sides, then spread a thin layer of the chocolate-hazelnut spread over one side of each slice and put them, spread-sides up, on a baking sheet.

2 Divide the strawberries over the spread and broil 1 minute, or until the strawberries are just warm. Dust with powdered sugar and serve hot.

1 loaf of ciabatta, preferably 1 day old, cut into 8 or 12 slices, each about $1/2$in. thick
$1/4$ cup chocolate-hazelnut spread
12oz. (about $2^1/4$ cups) strawberries, hulled and thickly sliced
1 tsp. powdered sugar, to serve

honey-flavored waffles with hot plums

Frozen waffles make a crisp and delicious base for warm plums when they are broiled and flavored with honey.

1 Preheat the broiler to high and preheat a ridged, cast-iron griddle pan or heavy-bottomed skillet over medium heat. Put the plums in the pan, cut-sides down, and cook 1 to 2 minutes, turning once, until warmed through. Set aside, covered, to keep warm.

2 Put the waffles on a broiler pan and brush the tops with a little of the melted butter. Broil 1 to 2 minutes until golden and crisp, then turn them over, brush with the remaining butter, and broil another 1 to 2 minutes. Drizzle 2 tablespoons of the honey over the waffles and broil 1 minute or until the honey bubbles slightly.

3 Transfer the waffles to plates and top with the plums. Drizzle with the remaining honey and serve hot with whipped cream.

4 large firm plums, quartered and pitted
4 large frozen waffles
1 tbsp. melted butter
6 tbsp. honey
whipped cream or vanilla ice cream, to serve

broiled figs with cheese & honey

Aromatic cardamom-scented honey lifts the sweet/sharp flavor combination of figs and goat cheese to a new level.

⌒m pods,

4 ⌒   figs,
  halved ⌒⌒ ⌒ise
1 tsp. powdered sugar
4oz. log fresh goat cheese, cut
  into 4 slices

1 Preheat the broiler to high and line a broiler pan with foil. Meanwhile, put the cardamom seeds, honey, and 1 tablespoon water in a small saucepan and bring to a boil over high heat, stirring. Let bubble 30 seconds, then remove from the heat and set aside to infuse.

2 Put the figs on the broiler pan, cut-sides up, and dust with the powdered sugar. Put the pan as close as possible to the heat source and broil 3 minutes or until the sugar bubbles and the figs soften slightly. Meanwhile, divide the cheese onto four plates.

3 Top the cheese with the figs and spoon the cardamom-infused honey, including the seeds, over them. Serve immediately.

broiled navel oranges with vanilla crusts

Vanilla sugar is very quick and easy to prepare, and it makes an aromatic crust for sweet navel oranges.

4 large navel oranges, cut in half
  horizontally
1/4 cup orange-flavored liqueur,
  such as Cointreau (optional)
1 tbsp. butter, chilled
crème fraîche, to serve

VANILLA SUGAR:
1/2 vanilla bean, cut into 4 pieces
1/4 cup granulated sugar

1 Preheat the broiler to high and line a baking sheet with foil. To make the vanilla sugar, put the vanilla bean pieces in a food processor or mini chopper and pulse 3 or 4 times to chop. Add the granulated sugar and blend 1 minute until well combined and the vanilla bean is finely chopped, then set aside.

2 Put the orange halves on the baking sheet, cut-sides up, trimming away a small sliver of peel from the bottom of each one so that they rest flat. Sprinkle with the liqueur, if using, then sprinkle evenly with the vanilla sugar. Cut the butter into four equal pieces and put 1 piece on top of each orange half.

3 Broil 7 to 8 minutes until the sugar is bubbling, then serve hot with crème fraîche for spooning over.

fast berry ice cream

This is the fastest, freshest, and most flavorful ice cream you will ever taste!

1/2 cup heavy cream
4 cups frozen mixed berries
1/4 cup granulated sugar
crisp cookies, such as plain rolled
   wafers, to serve

1 Put the cream in a medium bowl and beat, using an electric mixer, until soft peaks form, then set aside. Put the berries and granulated sugar in a food processor and blend 1 to 2 minutes until the mixture looks like large crystals. Stop and scrape down the sides of the food processor bowl as necessary.

2 Add the cream and blend another 2 minutes until smooth. You may need to stop and scrape down the sides of the bowl halfway through. Immediately spoon the ice cream into four bowls or glasses and serve with crisp cookies.

apricot & amaretto creams

Apricots have a slightly almond flavor, so this indulgent amaretto-flavored cream is a perfect accompaniment to the succulent summer fruit.

1 Preheat the broiler to high. Put the cream, powdered sugar, and vanilla extract in a medium bowl and beat, using an electric mixer, until soft peaks form. Add the amaretto and whisk until just combined. Be careful not to overmix.

2 Put the apricots on a baking sheet, cut-sides down, and broil 1 minute. Turn them over and broil another 1 to 2 minutes until they are warmed through.

3 Divide the apricots onto four plates and top with the cream. Sprinkle with slivered almonds and serve.

1/2 cup heavy cream
2 tsp. powdered sugar
1/4 tsp. vanilla extract
2 tbsp. amaretto liqueur
4 large or 8 small apricots, halved and pitted
1 tbsp. slivered almonds, to serve

bananas foster

Flambéeing, or flaming, is an impressive way to make a dessert really stand out—and it's easier than you might think.

1 Melt the butter in a 12-inch heavy-bottomed skillet over medium heat. Add the brown sugar and cook, stirring, 2 minutes or until the sugar melts, then add the nutmeg. Bring to a boil and boil 2 minutes until the sugar has darkened slightly.

2 Add the bananas and cook 1 minute, then turn them over and cook another 1 to 2 minutes until softened. Remove the pan from the heat and set aside.

3 Put the rum in a small saucepan over medium heat until warm, then carefully ignite it with a match and pour it over the bananas, pouring away from you. Allow the alcohol to burn off and the flame to extinguish itself. (Alternatively, boil the rum 1 to 2 minutes until the alcohol evaporates, then pour it over the bananas.)

4 Divide the bananas onto four plates and drizzle with the sauce. Let cool slightly, then serve with whipped cream.

1/4 cup (1/2 stick) butter
1/4 cup packed light brown sugar
1/4 tsp. freshly grated nutmeg, plus extra to serve
4 slightly underripe bananas, peeled and cut in half lengthwise
1/4 cup dark rum
whipped cream, to serve

raspberry & hazelnut eton mess

Eton Mess is a divine, traditional English combination of cream, strawberries, and crushed meringues. This take on the classic is made with raspberries—and whips up in almost no time at all.

1/4 cup chopped hazelnuts
1 cup raspberries
1/4 cup hazelnut-flavored liqueur, such as Frangelico (optional)
1 cup heavy cream
1/4 tsp. vanilla extract
2 ready-made meringue nests or 4 meringues, broken into small pieces

1 Put the hazelnuts in a dry skillet and cook over medium heat, stirring frequently, 2 to 3 minutes until lightly browned. Immediately transfer to a plate and set aside to cool slightly.
2 Reserve 4 of the raspberries for decoration and put the rest in a bowl. Add the liqueur, if using, and crush lightly with a fork.
3 Put the cream and vanilla extract in a large bowl and beat, using an electric mixer, until soft peaks form. Fold the raspberry mixture and meringues into the cream, then spoon the mixture into four glasses or bowls. Sprinkle the toasted hazelnuts over the top, decorate with the reserved raspberries, and serve.

sweet & sour strawberries with white chocolate cream

Strawberries and balsamic vinegar are delicious together—and especially pleasing with a white chocolate cream.

1/4 cup balsamic vinegar
2 tbsp. light brown sugar
2/3 cup heavy cream
2oz. white chocolate, finely grated
1lb. (about 3 cups) small strawberries, hulled

1 Put the balsamic vinegar, brown sugar, and 2 tablespoons water in a small saucepan and cook over high heat, stirring, 2 minutes until the sugar dissolves. Bring to a boil and boil 1 to 2 minutes or until syrupy. Remove the pan from the heat, pour the syrup into a large heatproof bowl, and set aside to cool slightly.
2 Meanwhile, put the cream in a medium bowl and beat, using an electric mixer, until soft peaks form, then fold in the chocolate.
3 Gently stir the strawberries into the balsamic syrup and spoon the mixture into four glasses or bowls. Drizzle any syrup left in the bowl over the mixture and serve warm with the white chocolate cream.

insalata di sicily

Sicily is famous for its wonderful fruit, particularly lemons, which flavor the renowned limoncello liqueur used here. It adds a delicious, tart/sweet dimension to whipped cream.

2/3 cup heavy cream
1 tbsp. powdered sugar
finely grated zest of 1/2 lemon
2 tbsp. limoncello liqueur
1 heaping cup cherries, pitted, and stems removed
8oz. (about 1 1/2 cups) strawberries, hulled, and halved or quartered, if large
2 large peaches, preferably white, halved, pitted, and each half cut into 8 slices
4 mint sprigs, to decorate

1 Put the cream, powdered sugar, and lemon zest in a bowl and beat, using an electric mixer, until soft peaks form. Add the limoncello and beat until just combined.

2 Spoon the limoncello cream into four bowls and arrange the cherries, strawberries, and peaches over it. Serve decorated with mint sprigs.

grape compote

Demerara sugar's caramel tones make a flavorful syrup that complements the freshness of the grapes in this easy treat.

1 Put the demerara sugar, sherry, if using, and $^1/_2$ cup water in a large saucepan and cook over medium heat 1 to 2 minutes, stirring occasionally, until the sugar dissolves. Bring to a boil over high heat and boil 4 minutes or until syrupy.
2 Drop the grapes into the hot syrup and let bubble a few seconds, then remove the pan from the heat.
3 Spoon the grapes into four heatproof bowls or glasses and pour the syrup over them. Serve topped with whipped cream and sprinkled with a little extra sugar.

$^1/_3$ heaping cup demerara sugar, plus extra to serve
2 tbsp. sherry (optional)
8oz. (about 1$^1/_2$ cups) seedless red grapes
8oz. (about 1$^1/_2$ cups) seedless green grapes
whipped cream, to serve

berry banana splits

The fresh berry sauce in this banana split is a healthier and more colorful alternative to the usual chocolate sauce.

1 Remove the ice cream from the freezer and let stand at room temperature to soften slightly. Meanwhile, put the almonds in a dry skillet and cook over medium heat, stirring frequently, 3 to 4 minutes until lightly browned. Immediately transfer them to a plate and set aside to cool slightly.
2 Put the strawberries, blueberries, raspberries, powdered sugar, and lemon juice in a blender or food processor and blend 1 to 2 minutes until pureed. Pass the puree through a mesh strainer into a clean bowl to remove the seeds.
3 Peel the bananas, then cut them in half lengthwise and put them in four large bowls or on oval plates. Top each portion of bananas with 2 scoops of ice cream, then spoon the berry sauce over the top. Sprinkle with the almonds and serve.

2 cups strawberry or vanilla ice cream
2 tbsp. slivered almonds
4 large strawberries, hulled
$^1/_3$ cup blueberries
$^1/_3$ cup raspberries
2 tbsp. powdered sugar
1$^1/_2$ tsp. lemon juice
4 bananas

▶ rosewater & berry ripples

Fragrant rosewater gives this slightly unusual rippled dessert a distinctive floral flavor.

8 large strawberries, hulled
1/3 cup raspberries
2 tbsp. granulated sugar
1 tbsp. rosewater
1 cup heavy cream
2 tsp. powdered sugar
1 tsp. vanilla extract
3/4 cup Greek yogurt
4 pieces rosewater-flavored
  Turkish delight, chopped,
  to decorate

1 Put the strawberries, raspberries, granulated sugar, and rosewater in a blender or food processor and blend 1 to 2 minutes until pureed. Rub the puree through a mesh strainer to remove the seeds and set aside.
2 Put the cream, powdered sugar, and vanilla extract in a large bowl and, using an electric mixer, beat until stiff peaks form. Fold in the yogurt, then spoon the puree over the mixture and stir once or twice to ripple through slightly. Be careful not to overmix.
3 Spoon the mixture into four glasses or bowls and serve decorated with the Turkish delight.

cherry fools

Tinned cherries are a wonderful standby to have on hand for quick desserts. In this recipe, they are easily transformed into a creamy fool.

1lb. canned pitted black cherries
  in syrup, strained, with syrup
  reserved
2/3 cup cherry yogurt
2 tbsp. kirsch liqueur (optional)
1 cup heavy cream
1 or 2 drops of almond extract,
  to taste
slivered almonds, preferably
  toasted, to decorate
shortbread cookies, to serve

1 Put 1/2 heaping cup of the cherries in a blender and add the yogurt and kirsch, if using. Blend 1 to 2 minutes until smooth.
2 Put the cream and almond extract in a large bowl and beat, using an electric mixer, until stiff peaks form. Fold the cherry mixture into the cream.
3 Reserve 4 of the remaining cherries for decoration and divide the rest into four glasses or bowls. Top with the cream mixture and then drizzle 1 tablespoon of the reserved syrup over each of the fools. Decorate with the reserved cherries and almonds. Serve with shortbread cookies.

◄ kiwi fools

Kiwifruit are pretty when sliced, and their bright, tart flavor cuts through the richness of the cream in this fool.

1 Thinly slice 1 kiwifruit and set aside. Chop the remaining kiwifruit into chunks, put them in a blender, and blend 1 to 2 minutes until pureed. Add the honey and blend until just mixed.

2 Put the cream in a large bowl and beat, using an electric mixer, until stiff peaks form. Fold in the kiwifruit puree, then spoon the mixture into four small glasses or bowls. Top with the reserved kiwifruit slices and serve with crisp cookies, if desired.

5 large kiwifruit, peeled
$1/4$ cup honey
1 cup heavy cream
crisp cookies, such as shortbread
  or ginger snaps, (optional)
  to serve

griddled apples with cinnamon croutons

This easy, deconstructed version of apple charlotte comes together in minutes to make a fabulous dessert.

1 Remove the ice cream from the freezer and let stand at room temperature to soften slightly. Preheat a large, ridged, cast-iron griddle pan or heavy-bottomed skillet over high heat. Trim thin slices from the top and bottom of each apple, then cut each one horizontally into 4 slices. Remove the core from the center of each slice, using an apple corer or small, sharp knife.

2 Cut out 2 circles from each slice of bread, using a 2-inch round cookie cutter. Mix the granulated sugar and cinnamon together on a plate and set aside.

3 Put the apple slices in the griddle pan and cook, pressing down firmly, 3 minutes on each side or until softened. Meanwhile, melt half of the butter in a large skillet over medium heat. When it is foaming and slightly brown, add the bread slices and fry 1 to 2 minutes until golden brown. Turn the slices over, add the remaining butter to the pan and continue frying another 1 minute or until golden and crisp.

4 Transfer the croutons to the plate with the cinnamon sugar and press down so that the sugar sticks to the surface. Put 2 apple slices on each of four plates and top each portion with 2 coated croutons. Serve with the ice cream on the side.

1 cup vanilla ice cream, to serve
2 large apples, such as royal gala
  or braeburn
4 slices of white bread, preferably
  slightly stale
$1/4$ cup granulated sugar
1 tbsp. cinnamon
2 tbsp. butter

bananas in coconut cream

For a quick, Asian-inspired treat, try this popular dessert from Thailand.

1/2 tsp. cornstarch
1³/4 cups coconut milk
1 tbsp. granulated sugar, plus
   extra to serve
4 slightly underripe bananas,
   peeled and halved lengthwise
finely grated zest of 1 small lime,
   to serve

1 Put the cornstarch and 1 tablespoon water in a small bowl and stir until smooth. Put the coconut milk and granulated sugar in a large saucepan and bring to a boil over medium heat. Add the cornstarch paste and boil, whisking continuously, 1 to 2 minutes until the milk thickens slightly.

2 Reduce the heat to low, add the bananas, and cook very gently 4 minutes or until the bananas are tender. Do not stir, as the bananas might break up.

3 Carefully spoon the bananas into four bowls and spoon the coconut cream over them. Sprinkle with a little lime zest and serve warm with extra sugar alongside so that everyone can sweeten the coconut cream to taste.

mango, blood orange & basil salad

Herbs aren't often featured in desserts, but this recipe shows how they can brighten up something as simple as a fruit salad.

4 large basil sprigs
1/4 cup granulated sugar
4 large blood oranges
1 large or 2 medium mangos

1 Remove the tips and smaller leaves from the basil sprigs and set aside. Put the remaining leaves and stems, the granulated sugar, and 4 tablespoons water in a saucepan and cook over high heat, stirring, 2 to 3 minutes until the sugar dissolves. Bring to a boil and boil 3 minutes until syrupy. Remove from the heat and set aside to cool while you prepare the fruit.

2 Cut the peel and pith away from the oranges, using a small serrated knife, then cut the oranges into segments and set aside in a bowl. Peel the mango and cut the flesh away from the pit in long slices. Arrange the fruit on four plates or in glasses.

3 Strain the basil syrup through a mesh strainer into a clean bowl and spoon it over the fruit. Serve decorated with the reserved basil leaves.

banoffee pavlova

Banana, caramel, and ready-made meringues combine in
a wonderful pavlova that is great for all seasons.

1 Put the granulated sugar and 2 tablespoons water in a saucepan
   and cook over medium heat, stirring, 30 seconds to 1 minute or
   until the sugar dissolves. Bring to a boil over high heat and boil
   4 to 5 minutes until the syrup has turned a medium caramel color.
   Remove from the heat and stir in $^1/_3$ cup of the cream, being very
   careful because it may sputter a bit.

2 Return the pan to a low heat and cook, stirring, 1 to 2 minutes
   until any hard lumps of caramel have dissolved, then keep warm
   over very low heat.

3 Put the remaining cream in a large bowl and beat, using an
   electric mixer, until soft peaks form. Peel and slice the bananas.

4 Put the meringue nests on four plates and spoon the whipped
   cream over them. Top with the banana slices, drizzle with the
   sauce, and serve. Alternatively, crumble the meringues into four
   glasses. Layer them with cream, bananas, and sauce and serve.

$^1/_3$ cup granulated sugar
1 cup heavy cream
2 large bananas
4 ready-made meringue nests
   or 8 small meringues

tipsy ten-minute tiramisù

This egg-free version of tiramisù is made more decadent with the addition of creamy Irish whiskey.

2 tsp. instant coffee granules
2 tbsp. Marsala wine
1/4 cup dark chocolate chips
1 cup mascarpone cheese
1/4 cup Irish cream whiskey,
   such as Baileys
2 tbsp. powdered sugar
1 cup heavy cream
1/2 tsp. vanilla extract
8 lady fingers, each broken into
   3 pieces
1 tsp. cocoa powder, to serve

1 Put the coffee and scant 1/2 cup water in a shallow bowl and mix until dissolved, then stir in the Marsala wine and set aside. Put the chocolate chips in a food processor and pulse until finely chopped.

2 Put the mascarpone, Irish cream, and powdered sugar in a large bowl and beat, using an electric mixer, 1 minute until combined. Put the cream and vanilla extract in another bowl and beat until soft peaks form (no need to clean the beaters first), then fold it into the mascarpone mixture.

3 Dip half of the lady finger pieces in the coffee mixture and arrange them in the bottoms of four glasses or bowls. Spoon half of the chocolate, then half of the mascarpone mixture, over the lady fingers. Dip the remaining lady fingers in the coffee and layer again with the remaining chocolate and mascarpone. Serve dusted with the cocoa powder.

raspberries with marsala mascarpone

Tart raspberries and sweet Marsala wine prove a perfect combination in this delicious, creamy concoction.

12oz. (about 2 3/4 cups) raspberries
1/4 cup Marsala wine
1/4 cup powdered sugar
1 cup mascarpone cheese
1/4 cup heavy cream
4 mint sprigs, to decorate
crisp cookies, such as amaretti
   or cantuccini, to serve

1 Reserve 20 of the plumpest raspberries for decoration. Put half of the remaining raspberries in a bowl and crush lightly with a fork. Stir in the rest of the raspberries and the Marsala wine and powdered sugar. Let stand 5 minutes.

2 Meanwhile, put the mascarpone and cream in a bowl and beat, using an electric mixer, until just smooth. Strain any liquid from the raspberries into a small bowl and stir half of it into the mascarpone mixture along with the raspberries.

3 Spoon the mascarpone mixture into four glasses or bowls and spoon the remaining liquid over them. Decorate with the reserved raspberries and mint sprigs, then serve with crisp cookies.

tofu-chocolate puddings

This rich pudding has such a wonderful, creamy texture it's hard to believe it's dairy-free!

SERVES 4 TO 6
1 cup dark chocolate chips
1lb. silken tofu, drained
1/4 cup powdered sugar
1 tsp. vanilla extract
4 or 6 mint sprigs, to decorate

1 Put four large (8-ounce) or six small (5-ounce) freezerproof glasses or bowls in the freezer to chill. Put the chocolate chips in a heatproof bowl and rest it over a pan of gently simmering water, making sure the bottom of the bowl does not touch the water. Heat 2 to 3 minutes, stirring occasionally, until the chocolate melts. Remove the bowl from the heat.

2 Meanwhile, blot the tofu dry with plenty of paper towel, then transfer it to a blender. Add the powdered sugar and vanilla extract and blend 1 minute until smooth. Add the melted chocolate and blend again until just combined.

3 Spoon the pudding into the chilled glasses and freeze 5 minutes to firm up the texture slightly. Serve decorated with mint sprigs.

rum & raisin sundaes

Rum and raisin sauce is a classic favorite and with good reason—it is quick to make and a perfect addition to ice cream sundaes.

2 cups vanilla ice cream
1/2 pineapple, peeled, cored, and cut horizontally into 4 x 1/2 in.-thick rings

RUM & RAISIN SAUCE:
1/2 cup raisins
1/2 cup gold or dark rum
1/4 cup granulated sugar
1/4 cup heavy cream

1 Remove the ice cream from the freezer and let stand at room temperature to soften slightly. To make the sauce, put the raisins, rum, granulated sugar, and 1/2 cup water in a saucepan and cook over medium heat, stirring, 3 to 4 minutes until the sugar dissolves. Bring to a boil over high heat and boil 1 to 2 minutes until syrupy, then remove from the heat and let stand 5 minutes.

2 Meanwhile, put 1 pineapple ring in each of four bowls or on plates. Top each one with a large scoop of ice cream.

3 Stir the cream into the rum and raisin sauce and spoon it over the ice cream and fruit. Serve immediately.

chocolate-coconut ice cream sandwiches

You can easily transform store-bought cookies into a treat that dessert lovers of all ages will adore.

1 Remove the ice cream from the freezer and let stand at room temperature to soften slightly. Put the chocolate chips in a heatproof bowl and rest it over a pan of gently simmering water, making sure the bottom of the bowl does not touch the water. Heat, stirring occasionally, 2 to 3 minutes until the chocolate melts. Remove the bowl from the heat.

2 Spread the melted chocolate over the top of each cookie and sprinkle with the coconut. Put the cookies, chocolate-sides up, on a small baking sheet or a plate and freeze 5 minutes until the chocolate sets.

3 Turn 4 of the chocolate-coated cookies over and put a scoop of the ice cream on each one, then sandwich with the remaining cookies, chocolate-sides up. Serve immediately.

2 cups coconut or vanilla ice cream
1 cup dark chocolate chips
8 flat, round cookies
1/4 cup unsweetened flaked coconut

phyllo ribbons

Fried phyllo pastry makes a whimsical dessert. Here, it's absolutely delicious served with honey, pine nuts and ice cream.

1 cup vanilla ice cream
2 cups canola oil, for deep-frying
1/4 cup pine nuts
2 sheets of phyllo pastry
1/4 cup honey
4 mint sprigs, to decorate

1 Remove the ice cream from the freezer and let stand at room temperature to soften slightly. Heat the oil in a deep heavy-bottomed saucepan or deep-fat fryer until it reaches 350°F. Meanwhile, put the pine nuts in a dry skillet and cook over medium heat, stirring frequently, 2 to 3 minutes until lightly browned and toasted. Immediately transfer them to a plate and set aside.

2 Roll up the phyllo sheets lengthwise and cut, from the short end, into 1/4 inch-thick slices. Shake the slices open so they look like ribbons. Working in batches to avoid overcrowding the pan, drop 1 handful of the phyllo ribbons into the oil and deep-fry 1 1/2 minutes until golden. Remove from the oil, using a slotted spoon, and drain on paper towel.

3 Divide the phyllo ribbons onto four plates and top each portion with 1 scoop of ice cream. Sprinkle with the pine nuts and drizzle with the honey. Decorate with mint sprigs and serve immediately.

coppa di zuccotto

Zuccotto is an Italian layered, bombe-type dessert. These cups, or coppas, have all of the delicious flavors of their larger cousin but are ready much more quickly.

2 tbsp. slivered almonds
2 tbsp. dark chocolate chips
juice and finely grated zest
   of 1 orange
1 tbsp. brandy
1 1/4 cups heavy cream
1/4 tsp. vanilla extract
3 large chocolate muffins, cut into
   bite-size cubes
1 tsp. cocoa powder, to serve

1 Put the almonds in a dry skillet and cook over medium heat, stirring frequently, 2 to 3 minutes or until lightly browned and toasted. Immediately transfer them to a plate and set aside to cool. Meanwhile, put the chocolate chips in a small food processor and pulse until finely chopped.

2 Mix the orange juice and brandy together in a small bowl and set aside. Put the cream, vanilla extract, and orange zest in a large bowl and beat, using an electric mixer, until soft peaks form.

3 Put half of the muffin cubes in four tall glasses or deep bowls and sprinkle with half of the almonds. Drizzle with half of the orange juice mixture and spoon half of the whipped cream over the top. Repeat the layers, then serve dusted with the cocoa powder.

hot fudge sundaes

Who can resist cold vanilla ice cream and hot chocolate fudge sauce? With this version, the sauce is ready so quickly, resistance truly is futile.

1 Remove the ice cream from the freezer and let stand at room temperature to soften slightly. Meanwhile, put the nuts in a dry skillet and cook over medium heat, stirring frequently, 2 to 3 minutes until lightly browned and toasted. Immediately transfer them to a plate and set aside.

2 Meanwhile, make the sauce. Put the chocolate chips, cream, brown sugar, vanilla extract, and butter in a saucepan and cook over medium heat, stirring, 1 to 2 minutes until the chocolate is just melted. Remove from the heat and stir until smooth.

3 Divide half of the ice cream into four sundae glasses or deep bowls, then spoon a little of the sauce over each. Add a second scoop of ice cream to each glass, spoon the remaining sauce over the top, and sprinkle with the nuts. Serve immediately with crisp cookies.

2 cups vanilla ice cream
1/4 cup chopped mixed nuts
crisp cookies, such vanilla wafers,
   to serve

HOT FUDGE SAUCE:
1/2 cup dark chocolate chips
1/2 cup heavy cream
2 tbsp. dark brown sugar
1/2 tsp. vanilla extract
1 tsp. butter

panettone perdu

A sweet Italian fruit bread that is popular as a gift at Christmas, panettone provides the base for this delicious, comforting dessert.

1 Heat a 12-inch heavy-bottomed skillet over medium heat. Meanwhile, put the eggs, milk, granulated sugar, and half of the vanilla extract in a shallow dish and beat until well mixed. Put the cream, powdered sugar, and remaining vanilla extract in a bowl and beat, using an electric mixer, until soft peaks form, then set aside.

2 Melt the butter in the skillet. Dip the panettone wedges into the egg mixture, turning them to coat thoroughly, then fry 2 minutes on each side or until golden brown.

3 Transfer the panettone to plates and dust with a little extra powdered sugar. Serve hot with the berries and whipped cream.

4 eggs
1/4 cup milk
1 tsp. granulated sugar
1/2 tsp. vanilla extract
1/2 cup heavy cream
1 tsp. powdered sugar, plus extra
   to serve
2 tbsp. butter
4 thick wedges of panettone
3/4 cup berries, such as blueberries
   or raspberries, to serve

knickerbocker glories (see age 76)

CHAPTER THREE

15-minute desserts

For creative confections that take just a quarter of an hour, it's time to turn on the heat. Broiling is great when you want to add a beautiful warm finish to billowing peaks of meringue, as in Lemon Meringue Pots, or give an Orange Soufflé Omelet a gloriously golden crust. Poaching fresh fruits lends a delicate, fully flavored elegance to desserts such as Ginger-Poached Rhubarb with Real Custard. Deep-frying is another technique that can transform an after-dinner treat into something spectacular. Strawberry Samosas emerge in a flash from hot oil, their crisp, flaky pastry giving way to a soft, sweet, surprising filling. Or cool things off with festive Knickerbocker Glories for a classic ice cream sundae experience. Whatever you choose, these quick recipes are sure to win applause.

cheesey chimichangas with mango salsa

Chimichangas, filled and rolled tortillas, are popular street snacks in Mexico. This version is a sweet twist on the classic.

2 cups canola oil, for deep-frying
8oz. (1 cup) cream cheese
1 tbsp. powdered sugar, plus extra
    for dusting
1/2 tsp. vanilla extract
4 wheat tortillas or wraps

MANGO SALSA:
1 large mango, peeled, pitted,
    and cut into small cubes
juice of 1 large lime
1 tsp. powdered sugar
1/2 mild red chilli, seeded and finely
    chopped (optional)

1 To make the salsa, put the mango, lime juice, powdered sugar, and chilli, if using, in a bowl and toss well. Taste and add more sugar, if necessary, then set aside.

2 Heat the oil in a large heavy-bottomed saucepan or deep-fat fryer over medium heat until it reaches 350°F. Meanwhile, put the cream cheese, powdered sugar, and vanilla extract in a bowl and beat, using an electric mixer, 1 minute until just combined. Put one-quarter of the cream cheese in the center of 1 tortilla. Fold in the sides of the tortilla and then roll up from the bottom to enclose the filling. Secure the tortilla with a wooden toothpick, then repeat with the remaining filling and tortillas.

3 Working in batches, if necessary, to avoid overcrowding the pan, fry the chimichangas 2 to 3 minutes or until golden brown and crisp, turning once halfway through. Remove from the oil, using a slotted spoon, and drain on paper towel. Return the oil to the correct temperature before each batch.

4 Dust with powdered sugar and serve hot with the mango salsa.

red berry mousses

This sweet, airy mousse makes a quick, delightful dessert.

1lb. raspberries (about 3 2/3 cups)
1/4 cup raspberry jam
    or red currant jelly
1 egg white
1 cup heavy cream
2 tbsp. powdered sugar
4 mint sprigs, to decorate

1 Chill four freezerproof glasses or bowls in the freezer. Put the raspberries and jelly in a blender or food processor and blend 1 to 2 minutes until pureed. Rub the puree through a mesh strainer into a clean bowl to remove the seeds, then set aside.

2 Put the egg white in a clean bowl and beat, using an electric mixer, until stiff peaks form, then set aside. Put the cream and powdered sugar in another large bowl and beat 2 to 3 minutes until soft peaks form (no need to wash the beaters first), then fold in the fruit puree.

3 Fold in the egg white, using a large metal spoon, then spoon the mousse into the chilled glasses. Serve decorated with mint sprigs.

cherries jubilee

Originally invented to celebrate Queen Victoria's golden jubilee, this flambéed dessert has stood the test of time.

1 Put the cherries, granulated sugar, and 1/2 cup water in a medium frying pan. If you prefer not to flambé (see step 4), add the kirsch to the pan. Cook over low heat, stirring occasionally, 6 to 7 minutes until the sugar dissolves and the cherries defrost. Bring to a boil over medium heat and boil 5 minutes, or until the liquid reduces by about half.

2 Meanwhile, mix together the arrowroot and 1 teaspoon cold water in a small bowl and set aside. Remove the ice cream from the freezer and leave to stand at room temperature to soften slightly.

3 Reduce the heat to low again and add the arrowroot mixture to the cherries. Cook, stirring continuously, 1 to 2 minutes until the mixture just thickens, then remove the pan from the heat.

4 To flambé the cherries, put the kirsch in a small saucepan over medium heat until warm, then carefully ignite it with a match and pour it over the cherries, pouring away from you. Allow the alcohol to burn off and the flame to extinguish itself. Serve immediately with the ice cream.

8oz. (about 2 cups) frozen pitted cherries
1/4 cup granulated sugar
1/4 cup kirsch liqueur
1/2 tsp. arrowroot
2 cups vanilla ice cream

blueberry & lemon brûlées

It's very hard to resist these delicious, individual brûlées.

1 Preheat the broiler to high and fill a small roasting pan with iced water. Spoon the blueberries into four 7-ounce ramekins. Put the yogurt, lemon curd, and lemon juice in a large bowl and mix until smooth. Put the cream in another bowl and beat, using an electric mixer, until soft peaks form, then fold it into the yogurt. Spoon the cream mixture over the blueberries and sprinkle with the granulated sugar.

2 Put the ramekins in the pan of iced water; the water should reach three-quarters of the way up the sides of the ramekins. Broil, as close as possible to the heat source, 1 to 2 minutes until the sugar melts. Remove from the heat and set aside 1 to 2 minutes to allow the sugar to set a little before serving.

1 1/3 cups blueberries
1/4 cup Greek yogurt
2 tbsp. lemon curd
1 tbsp. lemon juice
1 cup heavy cream
1/4 cup granulated sugar

▶ coconut snowballs

You don't need to wait for a blizzard to make these delightful, edible snowballs. For perfect ice cream balls, dip the scoop in hot water first.

2 cups coconut or vanilla ice cream
1/2 cup unsweetened flaked coconut
1 tbsp. powdered sugar
2 tbsp. chocolate chips
2 tbsp. unsweetened shaved or flaked coconut, preferably toasted

1 Line a baking sheet that will fit in your freezer with baking parchment. Divide the ice cream into 8 scoops on the parchment, then put the baking sheet in the freezer.

2 Set aside 1 tablespoon of the flaked coconut and put the rest in a dry skillet. Cook over high heat, stirring occasionally, 1 to 2 minutes until golden. Transfer to a plate, stir in the powdered sugar and reserved flaked coconut and set aside.

3 Put the chocolate chips in a heatproof bowl and rest it over a pan of gently simmering water, making sure the bottom of the bowl does not touch the water. Heat, stirring occasionally, 2 to 3 minutes until the chocolate melts, then set aside.

4 Remove the baking sheet from the freezer and put the ice cream balls on a plate. Sprinkle with the coconut mixture and drizzle with the chocolate. Sprinkle with the shaved coconut and serve immediately.

nectarines with honey zabaglione

This honey-flavored version of zabaglione, an Italian light custard made with Marsala wine, is perfect with summer stone fruits, such as nectarines.

4 nectarines or peaches, halved, pitted, and thinly sliced
4 egg yolks
1/4 cup granulated sugar
2 tbsp. honey
1/4 cup Marsala wine
crisp cookies, such as amaretti, to serve

1 Divide the nectarine slices into four large glasses or bowls and set aside. Put the egg yolks, granulated sugar, and honey in a heatproof bowl and rest it over a pan of simmering water, making sure the bottom of the bowl does not touch the water. Whisk, using an electric mixer, 1 to 2 minutes until pale and frothy. Add the Marsala wine and whisk continuously another 6 to 8 minutes until the zabaglione is thick and pale and has trippled in volume.

2 Spoon the zabaglione over the nectarines and serve immediately with crisp cookies.

strawberry samosas

Samosas are normally savoury, so filling them with juicy strawberries makes a nice, sweet change.

1 Put 1 sheet of phyllo pastry on a work surface and keep the rest covered with a clean, damp dish towel while you work. Fold the phyllo sheet in half lengthwise and then in half again. Position it vertically in front of you. Put one-quarter of the strawberries at the bottom end of the pastry, leaving a little space between the edges of the pastry and the filling. Fold the bottom-right corner of the pastry diagonally up over the filling to form a triangle, then fold the lower left-hand corner up the left edge, keeping the triangular shape. Continue folding to the end to enclose the filling. Seal with oil, if needed, then repeat with the remaining pastry and filling. Keep the samosas covered with the damp dish towel.

2 Heat the oil in a large heavy-bottomed saucepan or a deep-fat fryer until it reaches 350°F. Working in batches, if necessary, to avoid overcrowding the pan, fry the samosas 2 minutes, or until golden brown and crisp, turning once halfway through. Remove from the oil, using a slotted spoon, and drain on paper towel. Dust with powdered sugar while hot.

3 Warm the dulce de leche in a saucepan over medium heat until runny, then drizzle it over the samosas. Serve warm with ice cream.

4 sheets of phyllo pastry
4 large strawberries, hulled and cut into small cubes
2 cups canola oil, for deep-frying and sealing
1/4 cup dulce de leche or caramel sauce
powdered sugar, for dusting
1 cup vanilla ice cream, slightly softened, to serve

watermelon gazpacho

This is a wonderfully refreshing, fruity twist on the classic soup.

1 Put four freezerproof soup bowls in the freezer to chill. Working in batches, put the watermelon, strawberries, lime juice, and granulated sugar in a blender or food processor and blend 1 to 2 minutes until pureed. Transfer to a large bowl, mix well, and add more granulated sugar to taste, if necessary. Rub the puree through a mesh strainer into a clean bowl to remove any seeds. Thinly slice the reserved strawberries.

2 Pour the soup into the chilled bowls. Decorate with the sliced strawberries and mint sprigs and serve with meringues.

1lb. 4oz. (about 4 cups) peeled and chopped seedless watermelon, well chilled
1lb. (about 3 cups) strawberries, hulled and halved, with 4 whole strawberries reserved for decoration
juice of 1 large or 2 small limes
1/4 cup granulated sugar, plus extra to taste
4 mint sprigs, to decorate
ready-made meringues, to serve

indian mango with ginger & honey yogurt

Mango is a tender fruit that poaches very quickly. This recipe works really well with slightly underripe mangoes.

2 large, slightly underripe mangoes
1/4 cup granulated sugar
6 cardamom pods

GINGER & HONEY YOGURT:
2/3 cup plain yogurt
1/2 tsp. grated ginger root
1 tsp. honey, or to taste

1 Peel the mangoes and cut the flesh away from the pits in long slices, then set aside.

2 Put the granulated sugar, cardamom, and 1/2 cup water in a saucepan and cook over medium heat, stirring occasionally, 1 to 2 minutes until the sugar dissolves. Bring the syrup to a boil over high heat and add the mango slices. Immediately reduce the heat as low as possible and poach 3 to 5 minutes until tender.

3 Transfer the mango slices to four plates or bowls, using a slotted spoon. Increase the heat to high and return the syrup to a boil. Boil 2 to 3 minutes or until reduced by half. Remove from the heat and set aside to cool slightly.

4 Meanwhile, put the yogurt in a bowl and stir in the ginger and honey, adding more honey to taste, if desired. Spoon the syrup over the mango slices and serve with the yogurt.

fruit cups

The sauce for this fruit salad is similar to a punch-type cocktail and reminiscent of long summer afternoons.

1/4 cup red vermouth
1/4 cup orange juice
2 tbsp. gin
1 tbsp. granulated sugar
2 large oranges
8oz. (about 1 1/2 cups)
  strawberries, hulled and halved
  or quartered, if large
1/4 honeydew or other green
  melon, peeled, seeded and
  cut into bite-size chunks
2 heaping cups raspberries
1/4 cup lemonade or ginger ale
4 mint sprigs, to decorate

1 Fill a sink with 4 inches of iced water. Put the vermouth, orange juice, gin, and granulated sugar in a saucepan over medium heat and cook, stirring, 1 to 2 minutes or until the sugar dissolves. Bring to a boil over high heat and boil 1 to 2 minutes until the alcohol evaporates. Remove the pan from the heat, put it in the iced water, and let cool, stirring occasionally.

2 Meanwhile, cut the peel and pith from the oranges, using a small serrated knife. Cut the orange into segments and put them in a large bowl. Add the strawberries, melon, and raspberries.

3 Stir the lemonade into the syrup, then pour it over the fruit. Mix gently, then spoon the mixture into four tall glasses or deep bowls. Serve decorated with mint sprigs.

thai tropical fruit salad with sweet chili syrup

Dressed with sweet chili syrup, this fruit salad has a little kick.

1   To make the syrup, put the sweet chili sauce, powdered sugar, and 1 tablespoon water in a large bowl and stir until the sugar dissolves, then set aside.

2   Cut the pineapple into bite-size chunks, cutting on a lipped plate to catch and reserve the juice that is released. Add the pineapple and juice to the syrup, then add the mango and papaya. Peel the lychees, then peel the flesh away from the pits, adding the flesh to the bowl as you peel. Toss the fruit in the syrup.

3   Transfer the salad to four glasses or bowls. Serve decorated with mint leaves and with lime wedges for squeezing over.

1/4 large pineappl
   and cored
1 large mango, peeled, pitted,
   and cut into bite-size chunks
1 large papaya, peeled, seeded, and
   cut into bite-size chunks
8 lychees
mint leaves, to decorate
1 lime, cut into wedges, to serve

SWEET CHILI SYRUP:
1 tbsp. bottled sweet chili sauce
1 tbsp. powdered sugar

star fruit with ginger-thyme syrup

Star fruit look beautiful when sliced, and they make a stunning yet simple fruit salad that's just delicious.

2 large star fruit, thinly sliced

GINGER-THYME SYRUP:
1/2 cup granulated sugar
6 large thyme sprigs, plus extra thyme leaves for decoration
1 1/2 in. piece ginger root, peeled and thinly sliced

1 To make the syrup, put the granulated sugar, thyme sprigs, ginger, and 1/2 cup water in a small saucepan and cook over medium heat, stirring frequently, 2 minutes until the sugar dissolves. Bring to a boil over high heat and boil 2 minutes until slightly syrupy. Remove from the heat, stir in the star fruit, and set aside to infuse 5 minutes.
2 Remove the star fruit from the syrup, using a slotted spoon, and arrange on four plates or in bowls. Strain the syrup through a mesh strainer over the star fruit and serve decorated with extra thyme leaves.

pineapple strudel

A strudel can be quick to make using phyllo pastry, and a fruit such as pineapple that doesn't need lengthy cooking.

2 tbsp. butter, melted
1/2 pineapple, peeled, cored, and cut into 1/2 in. cubes
2 tbsp. granulated sugar
4 sheets of phyllo pastry, thawed if frozen
1 tsp. powdered sugar, for dusting
whipped cream, to serve

1 Preheat the oven to 450°F and brush a baking sheet generously with some of the melted butter. Toss the pineapple and granulated sugar together in a bowl.
2 Put 1 sheet of phyllo pastry on a work surface and keep the rest covered with a clean, damp dish towel while you work. Generously brush the top of the phyllo sheet with butter, then layer another sheet on top of it, brush with butter and repeat with the remaining phyllo. Spoon the pineapple along one of the long edges of the pastry, leaving a 1/2-inch border at either end of the pastry. Roll up the phyllo from the filled edge, tucking in the short edges as you roll to enclose the pineapple.
3 Carefully transfer the strudel to the baking sheet and brush with butter. Bake 10 minutes or until golden brown and crisp. Carefully slide the strudel onto a serving plate, dust with the powdered sugar, and serve hot with whipped cream.

lemon meringue pots

Lemon meringue pie can take some time to make, but this crustless version is ready in minutes.

14fl. oz. canned sweetened
   condensed milk
2 eggs, separated
juice and finely grated zest
   of 2 lemons
1/4 cup granulated sugar

1 Put the condensed milk, egg yolks, and lemon juice and zest in a bowl and mix well. Divide the mixture into four 7-ounce ramekins and freeze 5 minutes.

2 Meanwhile, preheat the broiler to high. Put the egg whites in a clean bowl and beat, using an electric mixer, until stiff peaks form. Beat in the granulated sugar in a thin stream and continue beating 1 to 2 minutes or until stiff and glossy.

3 Transfer the ramekins to a baking sheet and spoon the meringue over them. Make peaks in the meringue, using the tip of a knife. Broil 2 to 3 minutes or until the meringue is browned, watching carefully because it can burn easily. Serve immediately.

rum-buttered pineapple

Pineapple combined with rum is a great combination when you want to transport yourself mentally to the sunny Caribbean.

1 Remove the ice cream from the freezer and let stand at room temperature to soften slightly. Melt the butter in a 12-inch heavy-bottomed skillet over medium heat. When it is foaming, add the pineapple and cook 4 minutes on each side until softened. Add the rum and cook 2 minutes until the alcohol evaporates. Put the pineapple on four plates and set aside.

2 Reduce the heat to low and add the brown sugar and vanilla extract to the pan. Cook, stirring, 1 minute or until the sugar dissolves. Spoon the sauce over the pineapple and serve immediately with the ice cream.

1 cup vanilla ice cream
2 tbsp. butter
1 pineapple, peeled, cored, and cut into 8 long slices
2 tbsp. dark rum
2 tbsp. dark brown sugar
1/4 tsp. vanilla extract

orange soufflé omelet

An airy, puffed soufflé omelet is a lot quicker and easier to prepare than a classic soufflé—and it's almost as light. This one is prefect for sharing at the end of a romantic dinner for two.

1 Preheat the broiler to high. Put the egg whites in a clean bowl and beat, using an electric mixer, until medium peaks form. Put the yolks in a separate bowl, grate in the orange zest, and add the marmalade and liqueur, if using. Beat together using the mixer (no need to wash the beaters in between).

2 Heat a dry 8-inch nonstick skillet with a flameproof handle over medium heat. Fold the whisked whites into the yolk mixture, using a large metal spoon. Melt the butter in the skillet, then gently spoon in the egg mixture, being careful not to knock out too much air. Cook the omelet 3 to 4 minutes until golden underneath and starting to set.

3 Meanwhile, cut the peel and pith away from the orange, using a small serrated knife, then cut the flesh into segments and put them in a bowl. Put the skillet under the broiler and broil 1 to 2 minutes until set and the top is browned. Gently fold the omelet in half and turn it out onto a large plate (or, cut it in half and serve on two plates, if preferred). Serve with the orange segments and cream.

SERVES 2
4 eggs, separated
1 orange
2 tbsp. orange marmalade
1 tbsp. orange-flavored liqueur, such as Cointreau (optional)
1 tbsp. butter
light cream, to serve

▶ ginger-poached rhubarb with real custard

For this classic dessert, the rhubarb poaches quickly when cut into bite-size pieces.

1 cup plus 2 tbsp. granulated sugar
1 1/2 in. piece ginger root, peeled and thinly sliced
1 lb. rhubarb, cut into bite-size pieces

REAL CUSTARD:
1 egg yolk
1 tbsp. cornstarch
2 tbsp. granulated sugar
scant 1 cup milk
scant 1 cup heavy cream

1 Put 1 cup of the granulated sugar, ginger, and 1 3/4 cups water in a large saucepan and cook over medium heat, stirring occasionally, 2 to 3 minutes until the sugar dissolves. Bring to a boil over high heat, then reduce the heat to as low as possible and add the rhubarb. Cook 10 to 12 minutes until tender. Do not boil or the rhubarb will break up.

2 Meanwhile, make the custard. Put the egg yolk, cornstarch, remaining granulated sugar, and 4 tablespoons of the milk in a heatproof bowl. Put the remaining milk and the cream in a heavy-bottomed saucepan and heat over medium heat 4 minutes until just boiling. Slowly pour the hot milk mixture into the egg yolk mixture in a thin stream, whisking continuously, then return the mixture to the pan and cook over low heat, whisking continuously, 5 to 6 minutes until thickened.

3 Spoon the hot rhubarb into four bowls and serve with the hot custard for pouring over.

cinnamon-caramel apples

Apples bathed in a slightly spicy caramel sauce make a simple yet delightfully indulgent dessert.

1 tbsp. butter
scant 1/2 cup granulated sugar
2 large green apples, such as Granny Smith, peeled, cored, and each cut into 8 wedges
1/4 cup heavy cream
1/4 tsp. cinnamon, plus extra to serve
Greek yogurt or crème fraîche, to serve

1 Melt the butter in a large nonstick skillet over medium heat. When it is foaming, add the granulated sugar and 2 tablespoons water and cook, stirring, 1 to 2 minutes until the sugar dissolves. Add the apples and cook 3 to 4 minutes, turning them over a couple of times, until they soften slightly.

2 Bring the mixture to a boil over high heat and boil 3 to 4 minutes, turning the apples frequently, until the sugar has turned a light caramel color.

3 Remove from the heat and stir in the cream and cinnamon. Transfer the apples to four plates or bowls and spoon the sauce over them. Cool slightly, then dust with a little extra cinnamon and serve with yogurt alongside.

▶ knickerbocker glories

The stripes in these sundaes resemble old-fashioned trousers, which inspired the name. They are always popular with children.

2 cups vanilla ice cream
1/4 cup dark chocolate chips
2 tsp. light corn syrup or golden syrup
1 tbsp. butter
1lb. (about 3 cups) strawberries, hulled
2 tbsp. powdered sugar
a squeeze of lemon juice
1/2 cup heavy cream
2 large peaches, halved, pitted, and each half cut into 6 slices
1$2/3$ cups raspberries
2 tbsp. toasted sliced almonds, to decorate
4 maraschino cherries, drained, to decorate

1 Remove the ice cream from the freezer and let stand at room temperature to soften slightly. Put the chocolate chips, corn syrup, and butter in a small saucepan and cook over low heat, stirring frequently, 3 to 4 minutes until the chocolate is just melted. Remove from the heat and set aside to cool slightly.

2 Meanwhile, put the strawberries, powdered sugar, and lemon juice in a blender or food processor and blend until pureed. Rub the puree through a mesh strainer into a clean bowl to remove the seeds. Put the cream in a bowl and beat, using an electric mixer, until soft peaks form.

3 Put half of the peach slices in four sundae glasses or deep bowls. Add half of the raspberries and spoon half of the strawberry sauce over them. Add a scoop of ice cream to each glass, then repeat the layers again. Top each sundae with whipped cream, then drizzle with the chocolate sauce. Decorate with the almonds and maraschino cherries and serve.

fruit tostidas

Baked flour tortillas or wraps make a quick, unusual base for these fantastic fruit tarts.

4 small flour tortillas or wraps
1 tbsp. butter, melted
1/2 cup white chocolate chips
2 tbsp. heavy cream
1 cup ricotta cheese, drained
1 tbsp. powdered sugar
1 tsp. vanilla extract
1lb. (about 3 cups) strawberries, hulled and quartered

1 Preheat the oven to 400°F. Brush the tortillas with the melted butter and put them on two baking sheets. Bake 8 to 9 minutes until golden brown and crisp. Meanwhile, put the chocolate chips and cream in a large heatproof bowl and rest it over a pan of gently simmering water, making sure the bottom of the bowl does not touch the water. Heat, stirring occasionally, 2 to 3 minutes until the chocolate melts. Remove from the heat and set aside to cool slightly.

2 Put the ricotta, powdered sugar, and vanilla extract in a bowl and beat, using an electric mixer, 1 minute until combined. Put the baked tortillas on four plates and spread the ricotta mixture over them. Sprinkle with the strawberries, drizzle with the chocolate sauce, and serve.

palmiers with irish cream shots

These delicious layered cookies are divine with rich Irish cream.

²/₃ sheet of ready-rolled puff pastry, about 6oz.
1 tbsp. honey
1 tbsp. granulated sugar
¹/₄ cup Irish cream whiskey, such as Baileys
2 tbsp. coffee liqueur, such as Kahlúa
¹/₂ cup heavy cream
¹/₄ cup milk

1 Preheat the oven to 400°F and line two baking sheets with baking parchment. Trim the pastry into a rectangle about 10 x 3 inches. Spread the honey thinly over the surface of the pastry, then sprinkle the granulated sugar over it.

2 Fold the long edges of the pastry inwards so that they meet at the center, then fold them in again. Finally, fold one long edge over the other, as if closing a book. Use a sharp knife to cut the pastry into ¹/₂ inch-thick slices to make about 20 palmiers.

3 Put the palmiers on the baking sheets and bake 5 minutes. Turn the palmiers over, rotate the baking sheets, and bake another 3 to 4 minutes until golden brown. Meanwhile, put the Irish cream, coffee liqueur, cream, and milk in a small saucepan and warm over medium heat, then pour into shot glasses. Serve the warm palmiers with the cream shots.

firecrackers

Firecrackers get their name from their shape, but they are also very snappy to make.

1 Put all of the ingredients for the dip in a bowl and stir until the sugar dissolves, then set aside.

2 Put the dates and coconut in a bowl and stir in the orange juice $1/2$ teaspoon at a time until the mixture just holds together.

3 Heat the oil in a large heavy-bottomed saucepan or deep-fat fryer over high heat until it reaches 350°F and preheat the oven to 150°F. Put 1 wonton wrapper on a clean work surface and dampen the edges with water. Put 1 teaspoon of the date mixture in the bottom left-hand corner, then roll the wrapper up diagonally from the filled corner. Pinch and slightly twist the ends of the roll to seal and make a Tootsie Roll shape. Repeat with the remaining wonton wrappers and filling.

4 Working in batches to avoid overcrowding the pan, fry the firecrackers 2 minutes, turning once, until golden brown. Remove from the oil, using a slotted spoon, and drain on paper towel. Dust with the powdered sugar and serve with the dip.

4 large pitted dates, finely chopped
5 tbsp. unsweetened flaked coconut
2 tsp. orange juice
2 cups canola oil, for deep-frying
16 wonton wrappers, thawed if frozen
1 tsp. powdered sugar, to serve

CHILLI-LIME DIP:
1 tbsp. lime juice
1 tbsp. bottled sweet chili sauce
1 tbsp. mirin
2 tsp. granulated sugar

classic crêpes

Thin, crisp pancakes with lemon and sugar always seem like a special treat, but they are quick and easy to make.

1 Preheat the oven to 150°F and heat a 12-inch heavy-bottomed skillet over medium heat. Put the flour, egg, milk, and salt in a blender and blend 1 to 2 minutes until well mixed, then transfer to a pitcher.

2 Grease the skillet with a little oil , then add enough of the crêpe mixture to thinly cover the base of the skillet, tilting it as you pour to get an even coating. Fry the crêpe 1 minute on each side until golden brown. Transfer to the oven to keep warm while you make the remaining 3 crêpes, greasing the pan with a little more oil between each one. Sprinkle with granulated sugar and serve warm with lemon wedges for squeezing over.

scant 1 cup all-purpose flour
1 egg
1 cup milk
a pinch of salt
sunflower oil, for frying
granulated sugar, to serve
lemon wedges, to serve

▸ salted peanut praline parfaits

You'll be amazed by how quickly you can whip up the praline in this recipe. Salted peanuts complement the caramel beautifully.

2/3 cup salted peanuts
2/3 cup granulated sugar
sunflower oil, for greasing
1/2 cup heavy cream
2 cups vanilla ice cream, slightly softened
2 cups caramel ice cream, slightly softened

1 Line a baking sheet with baking parchment, spread out the peanuts in a single layer in the center, and set aside. Put the granulated sugar and 3 tablespoons water in a small saucepan over a medium heat and cook 2 minutes, stirring occasionally, until the sugar dissolves. Bring to a boil over high heat and boil 3 to 4 minutes until it turns a caramel color. Immediately pour the caramel over the peanuts and spread it out slightly, using a lightly greased palette knife. Let cool 2 minutes, then carefully transfer the parchment to a cooling rack and let set in a cool place 7 to 8 minutes. Meanwhile, put the cream in a bowl and beat, using an electric mixer, until soft peaks form, then set aside.

2 Break the praline into large pieces and reserve 4 for decoration. Put the rest in a plastic bag and crush to large crumbs with a rolling pin. Divide the vanilla ice cream into four glasses and sprinkle with half of the crushed praline. Add the caramel ice cream, then the remaining crushed praline. Top with the whipped cream and serve immediately with the reserved praline.

pecan-maple moneybags

The drawstring-purse shape of these wontons gives them the "moneybag" name. This is an easy way to make bite-size "pies."

1 tbsp. butter, melted, plus extra for greasing
1 cup pecan halves, chopped
1/4 cup maple syrup, plus extra to serve
12 wonton wrappers, thawed if frozen
1 cup vanilla ice cream, slightly softened, to serve

1 Preheat the oven to 400°F and generously grease a baking sheet with melted butter. Put the pecans and maple syrup in a small bowl and mix well.

2 Put 1 wonton wrapper on a clean work surface and brush the edges with water. Put 1 teaspoon of the pecan mixture in the center. To make a drawstring-purse shape, bring the corners of the wonton wrapper together and pinch just above the filling to seal. Repeat with the remaining wrappers and filling.

3 Put the moneybags on the baking sheet and brush generously with melted butter. Bake 6 to 8 minutes until crisp and golden. Serve hot with ice cream and drizzled with extra maple syrup.

thai coconut pancakes

This street-food favorite from Thailand is so easy to make that it will surely become one of your favorites, too.

2 tbsp. sunflower oil, for frying
$^2/_3$ cup rice flour or scant 1 cup all-purpose flour
$^1/_4$ cup granulated sugar
2 eggs
$^1/_4$ cup sweetened coconut cream, plus extra to serve
$^1/_4$ cup raisins
$^1/_4$ cup flaked or fresh grated coconut

1 Heat 1$^1/_2$ teaspoons of the oil in an 8-inch nonstick skillet over medium heat and preheat the oven to 150°F. Put the flour, granulated sugar, eggs, and $^1/_2$ cup water in a blender and blend 1 to 2 minutes until smooth and the consistency of light cream. When the oil is hot, pour in one-quarter of the batter, tilting the pan to cover the base evenly.

2 Cook 1 to 2 minutes until golden underneath and set on top. Spread 1 tablespoon of the coconut cream over the pancake and sprinkle with 1 tablespoon each of the raisins and coconut. Fold the pancake in half, turn it out onto a plate, and keep warm in the oven. Repeat with the remaining batter and fillings to make 3 more pancakes, adding more oil to the pan before each one. Serve warm with extra coconut cream.

fruity french toast

Crisp brioche, fruity berry jam, and fresh cream mean that this twist on French toast is destined to be a hit dessert.

$^1/_4$ cup raspberry jam
8 thin slices slightly stale brioche, challah, or white bread
4 eggs
$^1/_4$ cup heavy cream, plus extra to serve
1 tbsp. granulated sugar
$^1/_4$ tsp. vanilla extract
2 tbsp. butter, for frying
powdered sugar, to serve

1 Spread the jam over 4 slices of the bread and cover with the remaining slices of bread. Trim off and discard the crusts, if desired, then set the sandwiches aside. Put the eggs, cream, granulated sugar, and vanilla extract in a shallow dish and mix well.

2 Heat a 12-inch heavy-bottomed skillet over medium heat. Put half of the butter in the pan and, while it melts, dip 2 of the sandwiches in the egg mixture, turning to coat on both sides. Add the sandwiches to the pan and fry 2 minutes on each side until golden. Transfer to a plate and cover to keep warm while you make the remaining sandwiches.

3 Cut each sandwich in half and serve dusted with powdered sugar and with extra cream.

brandy snap baskets

Thin, crisp brandy snaps are easily molded into baskets, which you can serve with a variety of delicious fillings.

1 Preheat the oven to 375°F and line two baking sheets with baking parchment. Fill a sink with 4 inches of iced water and grease the outsides of four upturned 7-ounce ramekins with oil. Put the granulated sugar, butter, and syrup in a small saucepan and cook over low heat, stirring occasionally, 3 to 4 minutes until all of the ingredients have melted and are blended.

2 Remove the pan from the heat and put it in the iced water 1 to 2 minutes, stirring the mixture continuously, until cool, then remove from the water. Stir in the flour, lemon juice, and ginger.

3 Drop 2 rounded teaspoonfuls of the brandy snap mixture onto each baking sheet, spacing well apart. Bake 5 to 6 minutes until golden, then remove from the oven and let cool slightly, about 30 seconds. Using a palette knife, lift the brandy snaps onto the greased ramekins and gently shape them around the ramekins, using your hands. Let cool 1 to 2 minutes, then lift off and put the baskets right-side up on four plates. Fill with ice cream, top with berries, and serve dusted with powdered sugar.

sunflower oil, for greasing
2 tbsp. granulated sugar
2 tbsp. butter
1 tbsp. light corn syrup or golden syrup
$1/4$ cup all-purpose flour
a squeeze of lemon juice
a large pinch of ground ginger
ice cream or whipped cream, to serve
mixed berries, to serve
powdered sugar, to serve

white chocolate & lime mousses (see age 96)

CHAPTER FOUR

20-minute desserts

With twenty minutes, you have time to turn on the oven and create some stunning yet briskly made baked desserts. Puff pastry prefers a high heat, so you can bake it quickly, then split and fill it to make a simple but special Summer Cream Slice. Mocha Baked Alaskas need only a brief blast in the oven to brown the marshmallowy meringue coating and warm the chocolate cake base—the coffee ice cream center stays firm to make a cool contrast. Or fry up a spectacular batch of Mini Doughnuts with Jam. No one will guess that these warm, sugared sweethearts are made from a speedy scone-type dough. For chilled desserts, whip up White Chocolate & Lime Mousses or Mango & Ginger Trifle. Whatever you choose, these desserts will make the meal one to remember.

ricotta turnovers

Ricotta makes a creamy filling for turnovers. If you've got a little extra time, serve these with a fruit compote, such as the Grape Compote on page 47, instead of the jam sauce.

1/2 cup ricotta cheese
2 tbsp. ground almonds
4 tsp. chopped candied citrus peel
2 tbsp. granulated sugar
1/2 tsp. vanilla extract
2 sheets of ready-rolled puff pastry, about 1lb. in total
1 egg, beaten
1/4 cup apricot jam
1 tsp. powdered sugar

1 Preheat the oven to 400°F and line two baking sheets with baking parchment. In a bowl, mix the ricotta, almonds, citrus peel, granulated sugar, and vanilla extract together and then set aside.

2 Cut the pastry into 4 squares, each about 5 1/2 square inches. Put them on a cutting board and brush the edges with some of the egg. Divide the ricotta mixture onto the squares, positioning it slightly off-center, towards the top right-hand corner. Fold the pastry over diagonally to make a triangle and enclose the ricotta. Seal the edges by pressing down with the tines of a fork, then transfer them to the baking sheet and brush with the remaining egg. Bake 12 to 15 minutes until golden.

3 Meanwhile, put the jam and 1 tablespoon water in a small saucepan and warm over low heat. Serve the turnovers dusted with the powdered sugar and with the warm jam sauce.

crispy wonton mille-feuilles

Wonton wrappers, more conventionally used in Chinese cooking, become very crisp when baked—and ideal for layered desserts.

2 tbsp. butter, melted
12 square wonton wrappers, thawed if frozen
1 tbsp. powdered sugar, plus extra to serve
1/2 cup heavy cream
1/2 tsp. vanilla extract
1/2 cup Greek yogurt
2/3 cup blueberries
8 strawberries, hulled and quartered

1 Preheat the oven to 400°F and generously grease two baking sheets with some of the melted butter. Brush both sides of each wonton wrapper with the butter, then dust one side with the powdered sugar and transfer them to the baking sheets, sugared-sides up. Bake 5 minutes until crisp, watching carefully because the corners can burn easily.

2 Transfer the wrappers to a wire rack and let cool 5 minutes. Meanwhile, put the cream and vanilla extract in a large bowl and beat, using an electric mixer, until soft peaks form, then fold in the yogurt.

3 Put 1 wrapper on each of four plates and top with a heaping tablespoon of the cream mixture and some of the berries. Repeat the layering once more and top with the remaining wrappers, sugared-sides up. Dust with extra powdered sugar and serve.

tea-poached prunes

Soft dried fruit cooks much more quickly than traditional dried fruit, so keep some in your cupboard. Prunes go well with the slightly citrus notes of Earl Grey tea.

1 Put the prunes, tea bags, granulated sugar, lemon zest, and 2$^1/_2$ cups boiling water in a large saucepan and bring to a boil over high heat. Boil 5 minutes until the sugar dissolves.
2 Reduce the heat to low, remove the tea bags, and simmer, covered, 12 minutes or until the prunes are plump and tender. Remove from the heat and remove and discard the lemon zest.
3 Spoon the prunes into four heatproof glasses or bowls with a little of the syrup. Serve with crème fraîche for spooning over.

1$^1/_2$ heaping cups soft pitted dried prunes
2 Earl Grey tea bags
$^2/_3$ cup granulated sugar
1in. pared strip of lemon zest
crème fraîche, to serve

peaches & pecans with quick sablés

Sablés are crisp cookies made from sweetened pastry. They go perfectly with the mellow flavors of peaches and maple syrup.

1 Preheat the oven to 400°F and line a baking sheet with baking parchment. To make the sablés, cut out 8 rounds from the pastry, using a 1-inch cookie cutter. Brush the rounds with the egg and sprinkle the granulated sugar over them in a thin layer. Transfer to the baking sheet and bake 10 to 12 minutes until golden brown and slightly caramelized on top. Transfer to a wire rack and set aside to cool.
2 Meanwhile, melt the butter in a large skillet over medium heat. When it foams and is slightly brown, add the peaches and cook 3 to 5 minutes, turning once, until beginning to soften. Add the pecans and maple syrup and bring to a boil over high heat. Boil 1 minute, then remove from the heat and gently stir in the cream. Spoon the peaches into four bowls and serve warm with the sablés.

2 tbsp. butter
4 peaches, halved, pitted, and each half halved again
2 tbsp. chopped pecans
$^1/_4$ cup maple syrup
2 tbsp. heavy cream

QUICK SABLÉS:
1 sheet of rolled pie crust, about 8oz.
1 egg, beaten
2 tbsp. granulated sugar

◄ mango & ginger trifles

Sweet mango and spicy ginger make fabulous partners here.

1 Put the grated ginger, powdered sugar, and 2 tablespoons water in a small bowl and stir until the sugar dissolves. Put the mango flesh in another bowl and stir in half of the ginger mixture and 4 teaspoons of the candied ginger.

2 Put the orange juice and ginger wine, if using, in a shallow bowl and mix well. Put the lady fingers in four glasses or bowls and drizzle with the orange juice mixture, pushing the cookies down into the liquid. Add the mango mixture and set aside.

3 Put the cream in a bowl and beat, using an electric mixer, until soft peaks form, then fold in the remaining grated ginger mixture and spoon it over the mango. Sprinkle with the remaining candied ginger and serve decorated with mint leaves.

1in. piece of ginger root, peeled and finely grated
1/4 cup powdered sugar
1 large mango, peeled, pitted, and cut into bite-size pieces
2 tbsp. chopped candied ginger
1/2 cup orange juice
2 tbsp. ginger wine, such as Stone's, or sweet sherry (optional)
8 lady fingers, broken into pieces
1 cup heavy cream
mint leaves, to decorate

buttermilk scones with quick raspberry "jam"

When matched with a warm jam-like mixture and billowing clouds of cream, scones makes a luxurious dessert.

1 Preheat the oven to 400°F and lightly dust a baking sheet with flour. Mix the flour and salt together in a large bowl. Rub in the butter until the mixture resembles breadcrumbs, then stir in three-quarters of the buttermilk and all but 2 tablespoons of the granulated sugar. Mix to make a slightly soft dough, adding more buttermilk, if necessary.

2 Turn the dough out onto a lightly floured surface and roll it out to 3/4 inch thick. Cut out 8 scones, using a 11/2-inch round cookie cutter. Re-roll the trimmings as necessary. Brush the tops with the remaining buttermilk and bake 12 to 14 minutes until risen and golden brown.

3 Meanwhile, heat the raspberries and the reserved granulated sugar in a saucepan over a medium heat, stirring occasionally, 2 to 3 minutes until the sugar dissolves. Bring to a boil over high heat and boil, stirring occasionally, 8 to 10 minutes until thickened. Serve the scones with the warm "jam" and whipped cream.

2 cups self-rising flour, plus extra for dusting and rolling
1/4 tsp. salt
1/4 cup (1/2 stick) cold butter, diced
2/3 cup buttermilk or 1/2 cup plain yogurt
1 cup granulated sugar
11/2 cups raspberries
whipped cream, to serve

fruit shortcake tart

A sweet scone mixture can be used to make a quick tart base, which is perfect for topping with summer fruit.

1⅓ heaping cups self-rising flour, plus extra for rolling
¼ tsp. salt
3 tbsp. cold butter, diced
2 tbsp. granulated sugar
6 tbsp. milk
1 cup mascarpone cheese
1 tsp. powdered sugar, plus extra for dusting
finely grated zest of ½ lemon
1 peach or nectarine, halved, pitted, and sliced
8oz. (about 1½ cups) strawberries, hulled and halved
1 cup raspberries
honey, for drizzling

1 Preheat the oven to 400°F. Put the flour and salt in a large bowl and stir well, then rub in the butter until the mixture resembles breadcrumbs. Stir in the granulated sugar and 5 tablespoons of the milk and stir to make a soft dough, adding the remaining milk, if necessary.

2 Transfer the dough to a sheet of baking parchment on a work surface and use a lightly floured rolling pin to roll it out into an 8-inch round. Lift the parchment and dough onto a baking sheet and bake 12 to 14 minutes until risen and golden brown.

3 Meanwhile, put the mascarpone, powdered sugar, and lemon zest in a bowl and beat, using an electric mixer, 1 to 2 minutes until smooth. Carefully transfer the baked tart base to a serving plate, using a fish slice or palette knife. Spread the mascarpone mixture over the base and arrange the fruit on top. Serve drizzled with honey and dusted with powdered sugar.

gingered seared pears

A blast in a hot pan and a good dose of warming ginger are quick ways to pep up simple pears.

¼ cup granulated sugar
1 tsp. ground ginger, plus extra to serve
1 cup vanilla ice cream
¼ cup (½ stick) butter
2 large firm pears, peeled, quartered lengthwise with the stalk left intact, if possible, and cored

1 Heat a dry large heavy-bottomed skillet over medium heat. Mix the granulated sugar and ginger together on a large plate. Remove the ice cream from the freezer and let stand at room temperature to soften slightly.

2 Melt the butter in the pan. When it foams and is slightly brown, roll the pear quarters in the sugar mixture to coat on all sides. Cook 3 minutes on each side, including the curved side, spooning over the pan juices, until tender and slightly glazed.

3 Transfer the pears to plates and spoon the pan juices over them. Dust with a little extra ginger and serve hot with the ice cream.

lemon-polenta cupcakes

Polenta, or cornmeal, gives cakes a fine, crumbly texture and yellow color. These cupcakes make a great gluten-free dessert.

½ cup (1 stick) butter, softened
½ cup granulated sugar
1 heaping cup ground almonds
⅓ cup instant polenta
½ tsp. gluten-free baking powder
1 tsp. vanilla extract
1 egg, plus 1 egg yolk
a large pinch of salt
juice and finely grated zest
   of 1 lemon
¼ cup powdered sugar
crème fraîche, to serve

1 Preheat the oven to 400°F and line a muffin pan with 8 paper cupcake liners. Put the butter, granulated sugar, almonds, polenta, baking powder, vanilla extract, egg, egg yolk, and salt in a food processor and blend 1 minute until combined. Add the lemon zest and 1 tablespoon of the lemon juice and pulse 2 or 3 times to mix. Spoon the mixture evenly into the cupcake liners and bake 12 to 14 minutes until the tops are browned and firm. Rotate the pan halfway through baking.

2 While the cupcakes are baking, mix the powdered sugar with 1 tablespoon of the remaining lemon juice to make a syrup.

3 Carefully lift the warm cupcakes out of the muffin pan, using a palette knife, and peel off the paper liners. Transfer the cupcakes to bowls, drizzle with the syrup, and serve with crème fraîche.

barbados creams

This taste of the Caribbean, with bananas, rum, and dark brown sugar, makes a festive quick dessert.

1 tbsp. white rum
1 tbsp. lime juice
1 tbsp. granulated sugar
4 bananas, peeled and sliced
1 cup heavy cream
1 tsp. vanilla extract
1 tsp. powdered sugar
¼ cup Greek yogurt
¼ cup dark brown sugar

1 Put the rum, lime juice, and granulated sugar in a large bowl and stir until the sugar dissolves. Add the bananas and toss them gently in the mixture to prevent discoloration, then let stand 5 minutes to soften.

2 Meanwhile, put the cream, vanilla extract, and powdered sugar in a bowl and beat, using an electric mixer, until soft peaks form. Fold in the yogurt and set aside. Put the brown sugar and 1 tablespoon water in a small saucepan and cook over medium heat, stirring occasionally, 2 minutes until the sugar dissolves and the mixture is just bubbling. Remove from the heat.

3 Spoon the bananas into four glasses or bowls and spoon any juices left in the bowl over them. Top with the cream and drizzle the brown sugar sauce over the top. Serve immediately.

summer cream slice

This quicker version of the classic mille-feuille is bursting with the sweet, sunshine-packed flavors of summer.

1 Preheat the oven to 400°F and line two baking sheets with baking parchment. Cut 4 rectangles from the pastry, each about 4¼ x 3 inches, and put them on the baking sheets. Prick all over with a fork, then carefully brush the tops with the egg. Bake 12 to 15 minutes until risen, golden, and crisp.

2 Meanwhile, put the cream, vanilla extract, and 1 teaspoon of the powdered sugar in a bowl and beat, using an electric mixer, until soft peaks form, then set aside.

3 Transfer the pastries to a cutting board, using a fish slice or palette knife, and use a small, serrated knife to split the pastry in half horizontally, then let cool slightly.

4 Put each pastry bottom on a plate, top with some of the whipped cream, and arrange the fruit on top. Cover with the top halves of the pastry, dust with the remaining powdered sugar, and serve.

1 sheet of ready-rolled puff pastry, about 9oz.
1 egg, beaten
¾ cup heavy cream
1 tsp. vanilla extract
2 tsp. powdered sugar, plus extra to serve
8oz. (about 1½ cups) strawberries, hulled and thinly sliced
1 peach, halved, pitted and thinly sliced
½ cup raspberries

cherry jalousies

The classic "shutter" puff-pastry pie is made here in miniature version, with juicy canned cherries.

1 Preheat the oven to 450°F and line two baking sheets with baking parchment. Lightly flour a work surface and roll out the pastry to about half of its original thickness. Cut out 8 rectangles, each about 4 x 3 inches.

2 Put 4 pieces of pastry on the baking sheets, brush the edges with some of the egg, and arrange 6 cherries on top of each rectangle. Make 3 or 4 vertical cuts in the center of each remaining piece of pastry, leaving the border of each piece intact, and position these over the cherries. Press the edges of the top and bottom pastries together to seal and brush the tops with the egg. Bake 15 minutes or until risen, golden, and crisp.

3 Meanwhile, put the reserved cherry syrup in a saucepan and bring to a boil over high heat. Boil 5 to 6 minutes until thick enough to coat the back of a spoon. Remove from the heat and stir in any remaining cherries. Serve the jalousies hot with whipped cream and the cherry syrup spooned alongside.

all-purpose flour, for rolling
2 sheets of ready-rolled puff
    pastry, about 13oz. in total
1 egg, beaten
1lb. canned cherries in syrup,
    drained and syrup reserved
whipped cream, to serve

plums in port

If you want to create a fabulous dessert but the fruit you have to hand isn't quite ripe, poaching is the ideal technique to use. A sweet, spice-infused port syrup goes beautifully with plums.

1 Put the port, granulated sugar, star anise, and 1 cup water in a saucepan and cook over medium heat, stirring occasionally, 2 to 3 minutes until the sugar dissolves. Bring to a boil over high heat and boil 3 minutes, then reduce the heat to very low.

2 Add the plums and simmer, covered, 12 to 15 minutes, turning halfway through, until tender.

3 Remove the star anise and transfer the plums into bowls. Drizzle with some of the cooking liquid and serve with crème fraîche and a little nutmeg grated over them.

1 cup ruby port
1 heaping cup granulated sugar
2 star anise
8 large plums, halved, pitted, and
    each half halved again
crème fraîche or Greek yogurt,
    to serve
freshly grated nutmeg, to serve

white chocolate & lime mousses

Fresh citrus and sweet chocolate meld into a delicious dessert.

scant 2/3 cup white chocolate chips
1 cup heavy cream
finely grated zest of 2 large
  or 4 small limes
juice of 1 large or 2 small limes
2 tbsp. powdered sugar

1 Put four 7-ounce ramekins or freezerproof glasses in the freezer to chill. Put the chocolate chips and 2 tablespoons of the cream in a heatproof bowl and rest it over a pan of gently simmering water, making sure the bottom of the bowl does not touch the water. Heat, stirring occasionally, 2 to 3 minutes until the chocolate melts. Remove from the heat and set aside to cool slightly.

2 Meanwhile, put the remaining cream in a bowl and beat, using an electric mixer, until soft peaks form. Add one-quarter of it to the melted chocolate and whisk until smooth, then fold the chocolate mixture and half of the lime zest back into the whipped cream.

3 Spoon the mixture into the ramekins and freeze 8 to 10 minutes until slightly firmed. Meanwhile, put the lime juice and powdered sugar in a small bowl and stir until the sugar dissolves. Remove the mousses from the freezer, sprinkle with the remaining zest, and spoon the lime syrup over them. Serve immediately.

apricot puff bites

These mini pastries, inspired by the Danish classic, use just a few simple ingredients that are easy to keep on hand.

all-purpose flour, for rolling
1 sheet of ready-rolled puff
  pastry, about 9oz.
1 egg, beaten
1/4 cup apricot jam
2 tbsp. powdered sugar

1 Preheat the oven to 400°F and line two baking sheets with baking parchment. On a lightly floured surface, using a lightly floured rolling pin, roll out the pastry to about half its original thickness. Cut out 12 rectangles, each about 4 x 3 inches, then brush the edges with the egg.

2 Put 1 tablespoon of the jam on one half of each rectangle. Fold the other half over to cover the filling and press the edges together to seal. Transfer to the baking sheets and bake 10 minutes or until risen, golden, and crisp. Meanwhile, mix together the powdered sugar and 1/2 teaspoon water to make a thick but pourable icing. Add more water, if necessary.

3 Serve the puff bites warm, drizzled with the icing.

bananas with pecan praline

Crunchy caramel-coated pecans give this dessert extra appeal.

$^1/_4$ cup granulated sugar
$^1/_2$ cup pecan halves
2 cups caramel or maple ice cream
$^2/_3$ cup dark or milk chocolate chips
$^1/_4$ cup heavy cream
4 bananas

1 Line a baking sheet that will fit in your freezer with baking parchment and put it in the freezer. Put the granulated sugar and 3 tablespoons water in a nonstick skillet and cook over medium heat, stirring occasionally, 1 to 2 minutes until the sugar dissolves. Bring to a boil over high heat and boil 4 to 5 minutes until the sugar turns a medium caramel color.

2 Add the pecans and boil another 1 minute, then pour the pecans out onto the cold baking sheet, spreading them out as much as possible. Let cool 1 minute, then lift the parchment onto a wire rack and let cool 4 to 5 minutes until set and brittle. Remove the ice cream from the freezer and let stand at room temperature to soften slightly.

3 Meanwhile, put the chocolate chips and cream in a small saucepan and cook over very low heat, stirring occasionally, 3 to 4 minutes until the chocolate melts. Peel and slice the bananas and arrange them on four plates. Sprinkle the pecans over the top, breaking up any that have stuck together, and top with the ice cream. Drizzle with the chocolate sauce and serve.

raspberry cranachan

Broiling the oats and sugar, rather than toasting them in the oven, makes this version of the Scottish specialty much quicker.

1 Preheat the broiler to high and line a broiler pan with foil. Mix the oats and sugar together and spread the mixture out on the foil. Broil 4 to 5 minutes, stirring frequently, until the sugar melts and the oats are lightly toasted. Watch carefully because the sugar can burn easily. Remove from the broiler and let cool 5 minutes.

2 Meanwhile, put the cream in a large bowl and beat, using an electric mixer, until soft peaks form, then fold in the whisky and honey. Stir the oat mixture and crumble up any large lumps.

3 Put half of the raspberries in four glasses or bowls and spoon half of the whipped cream over them. Sprinkle with half of the oat mixture, then layer again. Serve drizzled with extra honey and whisky and decorated with the almonds and extra raspberries.

$3/4$ cup rolled oats, preferably jumbo
3 tbsp. light brown sugar
1 cup heavy cream
1 tbsp. whisky, plus extra to serve
2 tbsp. honey, plus extra to serve
$1^2/3$ heaping cups raspberries, plus extra to decorate
1 tbsp. toasted slivered almonds, to decorate

crêpes suzette

This quick version of the classic French dessert always impresses.

1 Preheat a 12-inch heavy-bottomed skillet over medium heat. Meanwhile, put the flour, egg, milk, and salt in a blender and blend 1 to 2 minutes until well mixed, then transfer to a pitcher.

2 Grease the skillet with oil and pour in enough of the batter to thinly cover the bottom of the pan, tilting the pan as you pour to coat it evenly. Cook the crêpe 1 minute on each side, or until golden brown. Fold into quarters and transfer to a plate. Repeat while you make the remaining 3 crêpes, greasing the pan with a little more oil between each one.

3 Melt the butter in the pan. When it is foaming, stir in the marmalade and orange juice. Add the crêpes and cook 1 minute, then remove from the heat. Put the liqueur in a small saucepan and warm it over low heat, then carefully ignite it with a match and pour it over the crêpes, pouring away from you. Allow the alcohol to burn off and the flame to extinguish itself, then spoon the crêpes and sauce onto four plates and serve immediately with cream.

$3/4$ heaping cup all-purpose flour
1 egg
1 cup milk
a pinch of salt
sunflower oil, for frying
3 tbsp. butter
$1/4$ cup orange marmalade
2 tbsp. orange juice
$1/4$ cup orange-flavored liqueur, such as Grand Marnier
light cream, to serve

▶mini doughnuts with jam

Using self-rising flour instead of yeast in this dough cuts down on the time it takes to make these delicious doughnuts.

2 cups canola oil, for deep-frying
$^1/_4$ cup raspberry jam
$1^3/_4$ cups self-rising flour, plus extra for rolling
2 tsp. baking powder
5 tbsp. granulated sugar
$^2/_3$ cup milk

1 Heat the oil in a large heavy-bottomed saucepan or deep-fat fryer over high heat until it reaches 350°F. Put the jam and 2 tablespoons water in a small saucepan and bring to a boil over high heat. Boil, stirring occasionally, 1 minute until the jam melts. Transfer to small dipping bowls and set aside.

2 Meanwhile, put the flour, baking powder, and 2 tablespoons of the granulated sugar in a large bowl and mix well. Add three-quarters of the milk and stir to make a soft dough, adding more milk as needed. Turn out the dough onto a lightly floured surface and roll it out to $^1/_2$ inch thick. Cut out rounds of dough, using a $1^3/_4$-inch round cookie cutter, then cut out the center holes using a 1-inch cutter. Gather together and re-roll the trimmings, as necessary, to make 24 mini doughnuts.

3 Working in batches to avoid overcrowding the pan, fry the doughnuts 2 minutes until puffed and golden, turning once halfway through. Remove from the oil, using a slotted spoon, and drain on paper towel. Return the oil to the correct temperature between batches. Toss the doughnuts in the remaining granulated sugar and serve warm with the jam for dipping.

warm fig & honey salad

This honey-scented dessert is a great choice when you want to give a meal a sophisticated finale.

12 large soft dried figs
$^1/_4$ cup honey
2 strips pared orange zest
Greek yogurt, to serve

1 Put the figs, honey, orange zest, and 2 cups water in a saucepan large enough to hold the figs snugly in a single layer. Cook over medium heat 30 seconds or until the honey dissolves. Bring to a boil over high heat, then reduce the heat to low and simmer, uncovered, 15 minutes until the figs are tender. Remove the figs from the pan, using a slotted spoon, and arrange on four plates.

2 Remove and discard the orange zest from the liquid, then bring to a boil over high heat and boil 2 to 3 minutes until syrupy. Spoon the syrup over the figs and serve topped with yogurt.

lemon cheesecakes

Making mini cheesecakes in ramekins, rather than in a large cake pan, means they're ready to serve in minutes.

10 to 12 ginger snaps
3 tbsp. butter
8oz. (1 cup) cream cheese
1/4 cup Greek yogurt
1/4 cup powdered sugar
juice and finely grated zest
  of 1 large lemon
light cream, to serve (optional)

1 Put the ginger snaps in a small plastic bag and crush to fine crumbs, using a rolling pin, then set aside. Melt the butter in a small saucepan over medium heat, then remove the pan from the heat, add the cookie crumbs, and stir until well coated in the butter. Press the crumbs firmly into the bottom of four 7-ounce ramekins and freeze 5 minutes.

2 Meanwhile, put the cream cheese in a large bowl and beat, using an electric mixer, 1 to 2 minutes until smooth, then beat in the yogurt, powdered sugar, and lemon juice and zest until well mixed.

3 Spoon the cheesecake mixture into the ramekins and freeze another 5 minutes. Serve with a little cream, if desired.

almond-amaretti bombes

These bombes are a creative way to end a meal.

2 cups vanilla ice cream
1/2 cup slivered almonds
10 amaretti cookies
1 tbsp. amaretto liqueur, to serve

1 Remove the ice cream from the freezer and let stand at room temperature to soften slightly. Line a baking sheet that will fit in your freezer with baking parchment and put it in the freezer. Put the almonds in a dry skillet and cook over medium heat, stirring frequently, 3 to 4 minutes, until golden. Set aside 1 tablespoon of the toasted almonds for decoration and transfer the rest to a food processor.

2 Crumble the cookies into the food processor and blend 1 minute or until the mixture resembles coarse crumbs. Spread the crumbs out on a large tray or baking sheet. Scoop half of the ice cream into 4 balls, put them on the tray, and roll to coat in the crumbs. Use forks to help manoeuvre the ice cream balls.

3 Transfer the coated ice cream balls to the chilled baking sheet and return it to the freezer, then repeat with the remaining ice cream to make 4 more bombes. Add them to the chilled baking sheet and freeze another 5 to 10 minutes to firm up.

4 Divide the bombes into four bowls and serve decorated with the reserved almonds and splashed with a few drops of the amaretto.

chocolate freezer squares

Melted chocolate studded with fruits and nuts sets very quickly if popped in the freezer. This recipe uses a mix of milk and dark chocolate, but you can use all dark chocolate if you prefer.

1 Line an 8-inch square cake pan with baking parchment, leaving enough parchment to hang over the sides of the pan. Put the milk and dark chocolate chips, butter, and corn syrup in a heavy-bottomed saucepan and heat over low heat 3 to 4 minutes, stirring occasionally, until just melted. Do not allow the mixture to boil.

2 Remove from the heat and stir in the shortbread, pistachios, and raisins. Pour the mixture into the pan and immediately put it in the freezer 10 minutes until firm.

3 Lift the chocolate square out of the pan, using the overhanging baking parchment, then cut or break it into squares and serve. Store leftovers in the fridge.

SERVES 8
1 cup milk chocolate chips
1 cup dark chocolate chips
1/2 cup (1 stick) butter, cubed
2 tbsp. light corn syrup or golden syrup
4 shortbread cookies, each broken into 8 pieces
1/4 cup chopped pistachios
1/4 cup raisins

mocha baked alaskas

Coffee and chocolate make a great combination in this rich and indulgent version of a baked Alaska.

1 Preheat the oven to 425°F and line a baking sheet with baking parchment. Remove the ice cream from the freezer and let stand at room temperature to soften slightly. Cut 1 round from each of the brownies, using a 2³/₄-inch round cookie cutter and put them on the baking sheet. Sprinkle with the liqueur, if using.

2 Put the egg whites in a clean bowl and beat, using an electric mixer, until stiff peaks form. Whisk in the granulated sugar in a thin stream and continue whisking until stiff and glossy. Put 1 scoop of ice cream on each of the brownie circles.

3 Working quickly, spoon the meringue over the ice cream and use a palette knife to spread it all the way down the sides of the Alaskas, making sure the ice cream and brownies are completely covered. Make a few peaks in the meringue, using the tip of the knife. Bake 6 to 7 minutes until the meringue is browned. Dust with a little cocoa powder and serve immediately.

1 cup coffee ice cream
4 large chocolate brownies
1 tbsp. coffee liqueur, such as Kahlúa (optional)
4 egg whites
¹/₂ cup granulated sugar
cocoa powder, to decorate

monte bianco expresso

The espresso-strength coffee in these chestnut and chocolate treasures creates a dessert with kick.

1 Put the chocolate chips in a heatproof bowl and rest it over a pan of gently simmering water, making sure the bottom of the bowl does not touch the water. Heat, stirring occasionally, 2 to 3 minutes until the chocolate melts. Remove from the heat.

2 Meanwhile, put the cream, vanilla extract, and powdered sugar in a bowl and beat, using an electric mixer, until soft peaks form.

3 Put the coffee and 2 tablespoons boiling water in a large heatproof mixing bowl and stir until dissolved. Add the chestnut puree, granulated sugar, and melted chocolate and beat, using the electric mixer (no need to wash the beaters in between), until just combined.

4 Spread the chocolate-chestnut puree over the meringue nests and top with whipped cream. Serve dusted with cocoa powder.

2 tbsp. dark chocolate chips
¹/₂ cup heavy cream
¹/₂ tsp. vanilla extract
¹/₂ tsp. powdered sugar
1 tsp. instant coffee granules
¹/₃ cup unsweetened chestnut puree
2 tbsp. granulated sugar
4 ready-made meringue nests
1 tsp. cocoa powder, to decorate

baby banana muffins with maple whipped cream

These mini banana muffins with a cream topping are so delicious, they'll disappear in minutes.

1 small banana, peeled
2 tbsp. light brown sugar
2 tbsp. sunflower oil
1 egg yolk
1/2 cup self-rising flour
1/4 tsp. cinnamon
a pinch of salt
1/4 cup chopped pecans
1/2 cup heavy cream
2 tbsp. maple syrup, plus extra
   to serve

1 Preheat the oven to 350°F and line a mini muffin pan with 12 mini paper cupcake liners. Put the banana in a food processor and pulse until chopped, then add the brown sugar, oil, egg yolk, flour, cinnamon, and salt. Blend 1 to 2 minutes until just combined. Add the pecans and pulse 2 or 3 times to mix, then spoon the mixture evenly into the paper liners.

2 Bake 12 minutes until the muffins are risen and firm to the touch. Meanwhile, put the cream in a bowl and beat, using an electric mixer, until stiff peaks form, then fold in the maple syrup.

3 Serve the muffins with the whipped cream and drizzled with extra maple syrup.

ciocolatto in carozza

"In carozza" means "in a carriage" in Italian and is the term for a French toast sandwich. This version has a very indulgent filling.

8 thin slices of white bread,
   preferably slightly stale
4 squares of dark or milk
   chocolate, about 1/2oz. each
4 eggs
1 tbsp. granulated sugar
1/4 tsp. vanilla extract
2 tbsp. butter
light cream, to serve

1 Put 4 slices of the bread on a cutting board and put 1 square of chocolate in the center of each one. Cover with the remaining slices of bread and press down around the chocolate to seal well. Trim off the bread crusts, leaving a border of about 5/8 inch all around the chocolate. (Alternatively, cut out round sandwiches, using a 3 1/2-inch cookie cutter.)

2 Heat a large heavy-bottomed skillet over medium heat. Beat the eggs, granulated sugar, and vanilla extract in a shallow bowl and dip 2 of the sandwiches in the egg, turning to coat both sides.

3 Melt half of the butter in the skillet and, when it is foaming, add the egg-coated sandwiches and fry 2 minutes on each side until golden. Transfer to two plates and cover with two upside-down plates to keep warm while you make the remaining 2 sandwiches. Drizzle with cream and serve warm.

cinnamon twists with hot chocolate dip

This is a speedy take on Spanish churros. Although churros are usually eaten for breakfast, this flaky version makes a more-than-satisfying dessert.

1 Preheat the oven to 400°F and line two baking sheets with baking parchment. Mix 1 tablespoon of the granulated sugar with the cinnamon and set aside. Cut the puff pastry into 12 strips, each about $5\frac{1}{2}$ inches long and $\frac{5}{8}$ inch wide. Brush both sides of the pastry strips with the egg and sprinkle with the cinnamon sugar. Put them on the baking sheets, twisting each one 3 or 4 times. Bake 10 minutes until risen, golden, and crisp.

2 Meanwhile, to make the dip, put the cream and chocolate chips in a small saucepan and cook over low heat 2 minutes, stirring continuously, until the chocolate melts. Remove from the heat and stir in the vanilla extract, then pour the chocolate sauce into ramekins or small bowls.

3 Serve the cinnamon twists hot with the sauce for dipping.

$\frac{1}{4}$ cup granulated sugar
$\frac{1}{4}$ tsp. cinnamon
$\frac{3}{4}$ sheet of ready-rolled puff pastry, about 7oz.
1 egg, beaten

HOT CHOCOLATE DIP:
$\frac{1}{2}$ cup heavy cream
$\frac{2}{3}$ cup dark chocolate chips
$\frac{1}{2}$ tsp. vanilla extract

poires belle hélène (see page 121)

CHAPTER FIVE

25-minute desserts

In twenty-five minutes, you can turn out fantastic desserts in double-quick time—whether you want to end your meal on a light, fruity note or cap it off with something more decadent. Scrumptious Lemon Sponge Puddings come together with hardly any effort at all when you simply blend together all of the ingredients for the cakes in a food processor. Minutes later, they're baking in the oven, and your hands are free to make the sweet-tart sauce that will provide the perfect finishing touch. From light-as-a-cloud Passionfruit Floating Islands and sweet, succulent Summer Berry Shortcakes to airy Chocolate Soufflés and rich Black-Bottomed Lime Cheesecakes, you'll find the options here truly tantalizing.

sticky coconut rice with mangoes

Kao Niow Ma Muang, as this is called in Thailand, is a popular family dessert.

1 cup jasmine rice
scant 1 cup milk, plus extra as needed
1³/4 cups coconut milk
¹/4 cup granulated sugar
2 small mangoes, peeled, pitted, and cut into large slices

1 Put the rice, milk, and half of the coconut milk in a saucepan and bring to a boil over high heat, stirring. Reduce the heat to low, and simmer, covered, 20 minutes or until the rice is tender. Add a splash of extra milk if the mixture gets too dry.

2 Meanwhile, put the remaining coconut milk and the granulated sugar in a separate saucepan and bring to a boil over medium heat, stirring until the sugar dissolves. Cook 10 minutes, stirring frequently, until reduced to about 4 tablespoons.

3 Stir the coconut milk mixture into the cooked rice, then spoon the rice into four bowls. Serve topped with the mango slices.

hot banana soufflés

Quick and impressive, these soufflés are also low in fat.

melted butter, for greasing
¹/4 cup granulated sugar, plus 4 tsp. for dusting
2 large bananas, peeled
1 egg yolk
1 tbsp. lemon juice
3 egg whites
light cream, to serve

1 Preheat the oven to 400°F with a baking sheet inside. Generously grease four 7-ounce ramekins with butter and dust the inside of each one with 1 teaspoon of the granulated sugar. Put the bananas, egg yolk, lemon juice, and 1 tablespoon of the granulated sugar in a food processor and blend to a puree. Scrape the puree into a large bowl and set aside.

2 In a separate clean bowl, whisk the egg whites, using an electric mixer, until stiff peaks form. Whisk in the remaining granulated sugar in a thin stream, whisking continuously until the meringue is stiff and glossy. Stir one-quarter of the meringue into the banana puree to lighten it, then fold in the rest.

3 Spoon the batter into the ramekins, filling them to the brim. Level the tops with a palette knife, scraping off and discarding any excess soufflé batter. Bake on the preheated baking sheet 15 minutes until risen. Drizzle with cream and serve immediately.

fig tarts

For a quick and elegant dessert, try these delicious tarts.

1 Preheat the oven to 400°F and line two baking sheets with baking parchment. Cut out 4 rounds from the pastry, using a sharp knife and an upturned 4¼-inch-wide coffee cup or saucer as a guide. Transfer the rounds to the baking sheets and prick them all over with a fork.
2 Arrange 3 fig halves on each pastry round, cut-sides up, and brush the edges of the pastry with the egg. Bake 15 minutes or until the pastry is risen, golden, and crisp, and the figs have softened slightly.
3 Dust with powdered sugar and carefully transfer to four plates. Serve hot with crème fraîche.

2 sheets of ready-rolled puff pastry, about 1lb. 2oz.
6 large figs, halved lengthwise
1 egg, beaten
powdered sugar, to serve
crème fraîche, to serve

tropical baked alaskas

Tangy fresh pineapple is a great foil for sweet meringue in these mini baked Alaskas.

1 Preheat the oven to 425°F and line a baking sheet with baking parchment. Remove the sorbet from the freezer and let stand at room temperature to soften slightly.
2 Cut out 4 rounds of sponge cake, using a 2¾-inch round cookie cutter. Put the pineapple rings on the cake rounds and trim around the edge of the pineapple so it is the same size as the cake. Cut the trimmings into smaller pieces and pack them into the center of the pineapple rings, where the core used to be (you may not need all of the trimmings). Transfer the cake and pineapple stacks to the baking sheet and set aside.
3 Put the egg whites in a clean bowl and beat, using an electric mixer, until stiff peaks form. Whisk in the granulated sugar in a thin stream, whisking continuously until stiff and glossy.
4 Put 1 scoop of the sorbet on each pineapple ring. Working quickly, spoon the meringue over the sorbet and use a palette knife to spread the meringue all the way down the sides, making sure the sorbet and cake are completely covered. Make a few peaks in the meringue, using the tip of the knife. Bake 6 to 7 minutes, until browned. Transfer to four plates and serve immediately.

1 cup mango sorbet or ice cream
4 slices of loaf-type vanilla sponge cake
½ pineapple, peeled, cored, and cut horizontally into 4 thick rings
4 egg whites
½ cup granulated sugar

upside-down mango tart

Tropical fruits, such as mango, are a great choice for quick, upside-down tarts.

1 sheet of ready-rolled puff
   pastry, about 9oz.
2 tbsp. butter, melted
1 tbsp. granulated sugar
$1/2$ tsp. vanilla extract
1 large, slightly underripe mango,
   peeled, pitted, and cut into
   $3/4$in. slices
whipped cream, to serve

1 Preheat the oven to 400°F. Using a sharp knife and an upturned 8in. pie plate as a guide, cut out a circle from the pastry, then set aside.

2 Sprinkle the butter, granulated sugar, and vanilla extract in the bottom of the pie plate and cover with the mango slices, packing them closely together and trimming, where necessary, to fit. Gently lay the pastry over the mango, tucking it in slightly around the edges.

3 Bake 20 minutes or until the pastry is golden brown and crisp. Lay a serving plate over the top of the pie plate and, using oven mitts or a folded dish towel to protect your hands, carefully invert the pie plate to turn the tart onto the serving plate, fruit-side up. Reposition any loose pieces of mango, using the tip of a knife, then slice the tart and serve with whipped cream.

berry hob cobbler

This cobbler topping is steamed, rather than baked, speeding up cooking time and resulting in sweet little dumplings.

3 cups fresh or frozen berries,
   such as blueberries, raspberries,
   and blackberries
2 apples, peeled, cored, and thinly
   sliced
scant $1^1/4$ cups granulated sugar
scant 1 cup all-purpose flour
1 tsp. baking powder
a large pinch of salt
2 tbsp. cold butter, diced
6 tbsp. milk
$1/2$ tsp. vanilla extract
whipped cream, to serve

1 Put the berries, apples, and 4 tablespoons water in a deep skillet or wok with a lid. Set aside 2 tablespoons of the granulated sugar and add the rest to the pan. Bring to a boil over medium heat, then reduce the heat to low and cook, covered, 10 minutes until the juices run from the berries and the apples are slightly softened.

2 Meanwhile, put the flour, baking powder, and salt in a large bowl and mix well. Rub in the butter until the mixture resembles breadcrumbs, then stir in the reserved granulated sugar. Mix the milk and vanilla extract together, then stir it into the flour, 1 tablespoon at a time, to make a soft, slightly damp dough (you may not need all of the milk). Uncover the pan and drop teaspoonfuls of the dough onto the fruit. Simmer, covered, 15 minutes or until the dough is cooked through and the fruit is softened. Spoon into bowls and serve with whipped cream.

pink peaches with vanilla crème fraîche

For a light, pretty treat, try this fabulous summer dessert of peaches poached in a rosé-wine syrup.

3 cups rosé wine
1 1/3 cups granulated sugar
1 vanilla bean, split lengthwise
4 peaches, halved and pitted
6 tbsp. crème fraîche
1 tbsp. powdered sugar

1 Put the wine, granulated sugar, and half of the vanilla bean in a large saucepan and bring to a boil over medium heat. Cook, stirring occasionally, 2 to 3 minutes until the sugar dissolves. Reduce the heat to low, add the peaches, and simmer 15 minutes, turning over halfway through, until tender. Make sure the liquid doesn't boil.

2 Meanwhile, put the crème fraîche and powdered sugar in a bowl. Using the tip of a sharp knife, scrape the seeds from the remaining half of the vanilla bean into the bowl and mix well.

3 Remove the peaches from the pan, using a slotted spoon, and set aside to cool slightly. Discard the vanilla bean and half of the poaching liquid, then bring the remaining liquid to a boil. Boil 4 to 5 minutes until syrupy. Meanwhile, carefully peel the skins from the peaches and discard. Transfer the peaches to four heatproof bowls or glasses, spoon a little of the syrup over them, and serve with the crème fraîche.

berry-ginger crumbles

Berries cook quickly, so they're perfect for fast desserts. The spicy ginger topping here complements them beautifully.

1 heaping cup fresh or frozen blueberries
1 heaping cup fresh or frozen raspberries
1/4 cup granulated sugar
1 cup all-purpose flour
1/4 cup (1/2 stick) cold butter, diced
1 tsp. ground ginger
a pinch of salt
1/4 cup demerara sugar
vanilla ice cream, to serve

1 Preheat the oven to 350°F. Pack the berries into four 7-ounce ramekins and evenly sprinkle with the granulated sugar.

2 Put the flour, butter, ginger, and salt in a food processor and blend until the mixture resembles breadcrumbs. Add the demerara sugar and pulse 3 or 4 times to combine, then spoon the topping over the berries.

3 Put the ramekins on a baking sheet and bake 20 minutes, or until the filling is bubbling and the topping is golden brown and crunchy. Serve hot with ice cream.

black-bottomed lime cheesecakes

The lime and dark chocolate combination is slightly unusual but delicious. The chocolate in the cheesecake crust helps the graham cracker crumbs and butter firm up very quickly.

2¹/₂oz. graham crackers
  (about 20 crackers)
3 tbsp. butter
2 tbsp. dark chocolate chips
4oz. (¹/₂ cup) cream cheese
finely grated zest of 2 limes
juice of 1¹/₂ limes
2 tbsp. powdered sugar
scant ¹/₂ cup heavy cream

1 Put a baking sheet in the freezer to chill. Put the graham crackers in a plastic bag and crush to fine crumbs, using a rolling pin. Melt the butter in a small saucepan over medium heat, then remove from the heat and stir in the chocolate chips until melted. Stir in the cracker crumbs until well coated and press the mixture firmly into the bottoms of four 3¹/₂-inch loose-bottomed tart pans.

2 Put the pans on the chilled baking sheet and freeze 5 minutes. Meanwhile, put the cream cheese in a large bowl and beat, using an electric mixer, 1 to 2 minutes until smooth. Reserve a generous pinch of the lime zest for decoration and add the rest to the cheese, along with the lime juice and powdered sugar. Beat until just combined, then add the cream and beat 1 to 2 minutes until smooth and thickened. Spoon the cheesecake mixture over the graham cracker crusts and freeze 10 minutes.

3 Carefully loosen the bottoms from the pans and lift out. Dip a palette knife in hot water, wipe dry, and use it to transfer the cheesecakes to plates. Serve sprinkled with the reserved lime zest.

apple streusels

The streusel mixture in this version of a classic recipe does a time-saving double act, baking into both a shortbread-like base and a crumbly topping.

1 Preheat the oven to 400°F with a baking sheet inside. Put the flour, granulated sugar, almonds, butter, and salt in a food processor and pulse 8–10 times until the mixture resembles large crumbs. Be careful not to overwork the mixture or it will form a dough.
2 Divide three-quarters of the streusel mixture into four 7-ounce ramekins and press firmly into the bottoms. Sprinkle the raisins over the streusel mixture, then top with the apples, pressing down so the filling is below the rim of the ramekins. Sprinkle the remaining streusel mixture over the top.
3 Bake on the preheated baking sheet 17 to 20 minutes or until the topping is golden brown. Serve hot with cream.

scant 1 cup all-purpose flour
$1/3$ cup granulated sugar
2 tbsp. ground almonds
6 tbsp. ($3/4$ stick) cold butter, diced
a pinch of salt
$1/4$ cup raisins
2 apples, peeled and grated
light cream or vanilla ice cream, to serve

baked nectarines with almond crumbs

Amaretti cookies make a wonderful sweet and crunchy topping for ripe nectarines.

1 Preheat the oven to 350°F and grease a baking dish large enough to hold the nectarine halves upright in a single layer with melted butter. Put the nectarines in the dish, cut-sides up.
2 Put the cookies in a small bag and crush to crumbs, using a rolling pin. Transfer to a small bowl and stir in the almonds, granulated sugar, and butter. Press 1 teaspoon of the crumb mixture into the indentation in each nectarine (where the pit used to be) and sprinkle any remaining crumbs over the top.
3 Bake 18 to 20 minutes or until the nectarines are softened and the topping is browned slightly. Transfer to four bowls and serve with whipped cream.

4 small nectarines, halved and pitted
8 amaretti cookies
$1/3$ cup ground almonds
3 tbsp. granulated sugar
2 tbsp. butter, melted, plus extra for greasing
whipped cream, to serve

▶ passion fruit floating islands

The "floating islands" in this French favorite are actually clouds of quickly poached meringue. The sharp passion fruit sauce contrasts with their marshmallow-like sweetness.

4 wrinkly, ripe passion fruit, halved
2 tbsp. orange juice
1 tbsp. powdered sugar
1¼ cups milk
2 egg whites
¼ cup granulated sugar

1 Scoop the passion fruit seeds and pulp into a bowl. Stir in the orange juice and powdered sugar and set aside. Put the milk and 1¼ cups water in a saucepan and bring to a boil over medium heat, then reduce the heat to low. It should not bubble.

2 Put the egg whites in a clean bowl and beat, using an electric mixer, until stiff peaks form. Beat in the granulated sugar in a thin stream and continue beating until the meringue is stiff and glossy. Take 1 heaping tablespoon of meringue and use a second spoon to shape it into a quenelle, or egg shape, then drop it into the hot milk.

3 Working in batches to avoid overcrowding the pan, poach the meringues 2 minutes on each side, then transfer to four plates, using a slotted spoon. Serve with the passion fruit sauce.

ricotta, apple & raisin hotcakes

Ricotta makes these surprisingly speedy hotcakes light and meltingly tender.

½ large apple, cored
½ cup ricotta cheese
¼ cup milk
2 eggs, separated
a pinch of salt
1 tbsp. granulated sugar
¾ cup self-rising flour
¼ cup raisins
sunflower oil, for frying
Greek yogurt or crème fraîche, to serve
honey, to serve

1 Heat a 12-inch heavy-bottomed skillet over medium heat and preheat the oven to 150°F. Grate the apple into a large bowl and stir in the ricotta, milk, egg yolks, salt, and sugar. Fold in the flour and raisins. Put the egg whites in a clean bowl and beat, using an electric mixer, until stiff peaks form, then fold them into the ricotta mixture, using a large metal spoon.

2 Grease the skillet with a little oil. Working in batches, pour 3 tablespoons of the batter into the pan to form 1 hotcake, adding as many hotcakes as will fit in the pan. Cook 2 minutes until golden brown on the bottom, then flip over and cook another 2 minutes. Transfer the hotcakes to a plate and keep warm in the oven while you make the rest.

3 Serve topped with yogurt and drizzled with honey.

lime phyllo tart

Delicate phyllo pastry, tart lime, and rich sweetened condensed milk team up here to form a delicious, alluring tart.

3 tbsp. butter, melted
4 sheets of phyllo pastry
14fl. oz. canned sweetened
   condensed milk, ideally chilled
1 cup heavy cream
juice and finely grated zest
   of 3 large limes
1 tsp. powdered sugar, to serve
lime wedges (optional), to serve

1 Preheat the oven to 400°F and generously grease two baking sheets with some of the melted butter. Put 1 sheet of phyllo pastry on a work surface and keep the rest covered with a clean, damp dish towel while you work. Brush the phyllo with butter, then fold it in half, short end to short end. Brush with butter and fold again, this time long end to long end.

2 Cut the folded phyllo crosswise into 3 rectangles and transfer to one of the baking sheets. Repeat with the remaining phyllo and butter to make a total of 12 rectangles. Bake 5 to 7 minutes, rotating the baking sheets halfway through, if necessary, until brown and crisp. Transfer the baked phyllo rectangles to a wire rack and let cool slightly.

3 Meanwhile, put the condensed milk, cream, and lime juice and zest in a large bowl that will fit in your freezer and beat, using an electric mixer, until thickened, then freeze 10 minutes.

4 Put 1 phyllo rectangle on each of four plates. Spread half of the lime filling over the 4 rectangles, then layer again and top with a third phyllo rectangle. Serve dusted with powdered sugar and with lime wedges, if desired, for squeezing over.

25-minute desserts

muhallabia

You can serve this Middle Eastern version of rice pudding hot for a quick dessert, but it is also popular chilled.

1/4 cup ground rice
4 tsp. cornstarch
1 3/4 cups milk
scant 1/2 cup heavy cream
2 tbsp. granulated sugar
1 tbsp. orange flower water
1 tbsp. unsalted pistachios,
   chopped, to serve
2 tbsp. honey, to serve

1 Put the rice, cornstarch, and one-quarter of the milk in a large saucepan and stir until smooth, then whisk in the rest of the milk, along with the cream and granulated sugar. Bring to a boil over medium heat, stirring continuously, until the sugar dissolves.

2 Reduce the heat to low and simmer, stirring frequently, 20 minutes or until thickened.

3 Remove from the heat and stir in the orange flower water. Spoon the pudding into four heatproof bowls and serve sprinkled with the pistachios and drizzled with the honey.

poires belle hélène

This classic French combination of poached pears with rich chocolate sauce is elegant and quick.

1 Put the granulated sugar, lemon zest, and 3 cups water in a saucepan and bring to a boil over medium heat. Boil, stirring occasionally, 2 to 3 minutes until the sugar dissolves, then reduce the heat to low.

2 Meanwhile, peel the pears, leaving the stalks intact, and trim a small piece from the base of each of the pears so they can stand upright on a plate. Put the pears in the saucepan and poach in the syrup over low heat 18 to 20 minutes, turning halfway through, until tender. Make sure the liquid doesn't boil.

3 While the pears are cooking, make the chocolate sauce. Put the chocolate chips, cream, and vanilla extract in a small saucepan over low heat and cook, stirring, 2 to 3 minutes until smooth and the chocolate melts. Using a slotted spoon, transfer the pears to four plates and serve with the hot sauce spooned over them.

1 heaping cup granulated sugar
thinly pared zest of $1/2$ lemon
4 ripe pears
1 heaping cup dark chocolate chips
$3/4$ cup heavy cream
$1/4$ tsp. vanilla extract

▶lemon sponge puddings

These individual lemon sponges are coated in a satiny smooth lemon sauce.

1/2 cup (1 stick) butter, softened, plus extra for greasing
2/3 cup granulated sugar
2 eggs plus 1 yolk
3/4 cup plus 2 tbsp. self-rising flour
juice and finely grated zest of 1 large lemon, plus extra zest to decorate
a pinch of salt
2 tsp. cornstarch
crème fraîche, to serve

1 Preheat the oven to 350°F and grease four 7-ounce ramekins or molds. Set aside 2 tablespoons of the granulated sugar and put the rest in a food processor. Add the butter, whole eggs, flour, lemon zest, and salt and blend 1 to 2 minutes until just combined. Spoon the mixture into the ramekins and bake 18 to 20 minutes until risen, brown, and firm to the touch.

2 Meanwhile, make the sauce. Put the egg yolk, cornstarch, and lemon juice in a bowl and whisk well. Put the reserved granulated sugar and scant 1/2 cup water in a saucepan and heat over medium heat, stirring, 30 seconds or until the sugar dissolves. Whisking continuously, pour the sugar syrup into the egg mixture in a thin stream. Return the mixture to the pan and cook over low heat, whisking continuously, 2 minutes or until thickened.

3 Turn out the cakes and put them right-side up on four plates. Spoon the sauce over them and serve warm with crème fraîche and extra lemon zest to decorate.

summer tiramisù

Raspberry and orange give this speedy dessert a bright flavor.

2 eggs, separated
1/4 cup granulated sugar
1 cup mascarpone cheese
1/4 cup orange juice
2 tbsp. orange-flavored liqueur, such as Cointreau
12 lady fingers, each broken into 2 to 3 pieces
1 cup raspberries, plus extra to decorate
2oz. white chocolate, chopped
1 tsp. powdered sugar
4 mint sprigs, to decorate

1 Put the egg whites in a clean bowl and beat, using an electric mixer, until soft peaks form. Put the egg yolks, granulated sugar, and mascarpone in another bowl and beat, using the mixer (no need to clean the beaters first), until just smooth. Stir in a little of the whisked egg whites to lighten, then fold in the rest.

2 Stir the orange juice and liqueur together in a shallow bowl. Dip half of the cookie pieces into the liquid and put them in four large glasses or bowls. Sprinkle half of the raspberries over the top, then follow with half of the mascarpone mixture. Dip the remaining cookies and layer again with the raspberries and mascarpone, then sprinkle the chopped chocolate over the top.

3 Dust with the powdered sugar and serve decorated with extra raspberries and mint sprigs.

25-minute desserts

cherry clafoutis

The classic French dessert bakes quickly if you make it in individual ramekins.

1 Preheat the oven to 400°F with a baking sheet inside and grease four 7-ounce ramekins with oil. Divide the cherries into the ramekins.
2 Put the flour, granulated sugar, eggs, and milk in a blender and blend 1 to 2 minutes until well mixed and smooth, then carefully pour the mixture into the ramekins and press 1 fresh cherry, if using, into the top of each one. Bake on the preheated baking sheet for 20 minutes or until puffed and brown.
3 Dust the clafoutis with the powdered sugar, drizzle with cream, if desired, and serve hot.

sunflower oil, for greasing
$1^1/2$ cups fresh or frozen pitted cherries, plus 4 fresh cherries with stems for decoration (optional)
$1/3$ cup all-purpose flour
2 tbsp. granulated sugar
2 eggs
$1/2$ cup milk
1 tsp. powdered sugar, to serve
light cream (optional), to serve

summer berry shortcakes

Shortcakes are rich scones that are a popular American summer dessert when paired with ripe, juicy berries.

1 Preheat the oven to 400°F and grease a baking sheet with butter. Mix together the flour, baking powder, and salt in a large bowl. Rub in the butter until the mixture resembles breadcrumbs, then stir in the granulated sugar.
2 Put the egg and 4 tablespoons of the cream in a bowl and whisk well. Mix 4 tablespoons of the egg mixture into the flour, 1 tablespoon at a time, to make a soft, slightly damp dough, adding more liquid, if needed. Turn out the dough onto a lightly floured surface and roll it out to $1/2$ inch thick. Cut out 4 shortcakes, using a $2^3/4$-inch round cookie cutter, then gather up and reroll the trimmings and cut out 4 more shortcakes.
3 Transfer the shortcakes to the baking sheet and brush the tops with any remaining egg mixture. Bake 15 minutes or until risen and golden brown. Meanwhile, toss the strawberries, mixed berries, and powdered sugar together in a small bowl. In another bowl, whip the remaining cream, using an electric mixer, until soft peaks form. Serve the warm shortcakes halved and sandwiched with the cream and berries.

$1/2$ cup (1 stick) cold butter, diced, plus extra for greasing
scant 2 cups all-purpose flour, plus extra for rolling
2 tsp. baking powder
$1/4$ tsp. salt
2 tbsp. granulated sugar
1 egg
1 cup heavy cream
4 large strawberries, hulled and quartered
$1^1/4$ cups mixed berries, such as blueberries and raspberries
1 tbsp. powdered sugar

warm loaded oatmeal cookies

These cookies are packed with chocolate, nuts and raisins —flavors you won't be able to resist.

¼ cup (½ stick) butter, softened
⅓ cup granulated sugar
1 egg yolk
1 tsp. vanilla extract
¾ cup rolled oats
scant ½ cup all-purpose flour
¼ tsp. bicarbonate soda
a pinch of salt
¼ cup raisins
¼ cup chopped pecans or walnuts
2 tbsp. milk chocolate chips
ice cream, to serve

1 Preheat the oven to 350°F and line two baking sheets with baking parchment. Put the butter, granulated sugar, egg yolk, vanilla extract, oats, flour, baking soda, and salt in a large bowl and beat, using an electric mixer, until just combined. Stir in the raisins, nuts, and chocolate chips.

2 Divide the mixture into 12 equal portions, roll them into balls and put them on the baking sheets, then flatten to about ½ inch thick. Bake 12 to 15 minutes until golden brown around the edges. Remove the ice cream from the freezer and let stand at room temperature to soften slightly.

3 Slide the baking parchment and cookies onto wire racks and let cool 2 to 3 minutes. Carefully transfer the cookies to four plates, using a spatula to move them because they will be soft. Serve warm with ice cream.

caramel brioche puddings

A luxurious variation on everyday bread pudding.

2 egg yolks
2 tbsp. granulated sugar
1 tbsp. cornstarch
scant 1 cup milk
scant 1 cup heavy cream, plus
  extra to serve
¼ cup dulce de leche or caramel
  sauce, plus extra to serve
2 thick slices of brioche, torn into
  bite-size pieces

1 Preheat the oven to 350°F. Whisk together the egg yolks, granulated sugar, cornstarch, and 2 tablespoons of the milk in a large heatproof bowl and set aside.

2 Put the cream, dulce de leche, and the remaining milk in a saucepan and bring to a boil over high heat, stirring. Pour the mixture in a thin stream into the egg mixture, whisking continuously. Return the mixture to the pan, reduce the heat to very low, and continue whisking 3 to 4 minutes until thickened slightly. Add the brioche pieces and simmer another 3 to 4 minutes until the brioche absorbs some of the custard.

3 Spoon the mixture into four 7-ounce ramekins and bake 8 to 10 minutes until slightly puffed and just set. Serve with extra dulce de leche and cream for pouring over.

m'hanncha

The name of this Middle Eastern dessert translates as "the snake" because of its coiled shape.

1 Preheat the oven to 400°F and melt half of the butter in a small saucepan over medium heat. Grease a large baking sheet with a little of the melted butter and set the rest aside. Put the unmelted butter, almonds, granulated sugar, orange zest, and orange flower water in a bowl, mix well, and set aside.

2 Put 1 sheet of phyllo pastry on a work surface and keep the rest covered with a clean, damp dish towel while you work. Brush the pastry with some of the melted butter, then fold it in half, short end to short end, and brush again. Spoon one-quarter of the almond mixture along one of the long sides of the pastry, leaving a $1/2$-inch border at both ends. Fold the short sides in towards the center, then roll up the pastry from the almond end to enclose the mixture. Coil the pastry into a spiral and put it on the baking sheet, then brush generously with more melted butter. Repeat with the remaining pastry sheets, butter, and filling.

3 Bake 15 minutes or until golden brown and crisp. Dust with powdered sugar and serve hot.

$1/2$ cup (1 stick) butter, softened
$3/4$ cup ground almonds
2 tbsp. granulated sugar
finely grated zest of $1/2$ large orange
1 tsp. orange flower water
4 sheets of phyllo pastry
powdered sugar, to serve

chocolate cream pots

Smooth and rich, this classic chocolate dessert is a favorite with adults and children alike.

1 Put four 7-ounce ramekins or freezerproof glasses in the freezer to chill and fill a sink with about 4 inches of iced water. Put the egg yolks, cornstarch, granulated sugar, and 4 tablespoons of the milk in a large heatproof bowl and whisk until combined, then set aside. Put the cream and the remaining milk in a saucepan and cook over medium heat 2 minutes until just boiling.

2 Pour the hot milk mixture into the egg mixture in a thin stream, whisking continuously. Return the mixture to the pan and continue whisking over low heat 5 to 6 minutes until thickened. Remove the pan from the heat, add the chocolate chips and vanilla extract, and stir until the chocolate melts.

3 Put the pan in the iced water and whisk 5 minutes until cooled. Spoon the chocolate cream into the chilled ramekins and serve with crisp cookies.

2 egg yolks
1 tbsp. cornstarch
$1/4$ cup granulated sugar
scant 1 cup whole milk
scant 1 cup heavy cream
$1/2$ cup dark chocolate chips
$1/2$ tsp. vanilla extract
crisp cookies, such as thin butter cookies or shortbread, to serve

arroz con leches

Originating from Latin America, this simple dish of rice with milk has become popular around the world.

1 Put the rice, both milks, and the vanilla bean in a saucepan and bring to a boil over medium heat, stirring occasionally. Reduce the heat to low and simmer 20 minutes or until the rice is tender. Stir every 5 minutes to prevent the rice from sticking to the bottom of the pan. Remove from the heat.

2 Using the back of a knife, scrape out the seeds from the vanilla bean and add them back to the saucepan, then stir in the granulated sugar to taste.

3 Divide the rice into four bowls and drizzle with the dulce de leche and serve warm.

$1/2$ cup risotto rice, such as arborio
5fl. oz. canned evaporated milk
2 cups milk
1 vanilla bean, halved lengthwise
2 to 3 tbsp. granulated sugar
$1/4$ cup dulce de leche or caramel sauce, to serve

butterscotch pudding

This unusual, delicious pudding comes from everyday ingredients.

3 eggs, separated
2 tbsp. cornstarch
1 cup milk
1 cup packed light brown sugar
6 tbsp. (3/4 stick) butter
1 tsp. vanilla extract
1 1/2 cups fresh white breadcrumbs
a pinch of salt
1/4 cup granulated sugar

1 Preheat the oven to 400°F. Whisk the egg yolks, cornstarch, and 3 tablespoons of the milk together in a large bowl and set aside. Put the brown sugar, butter, and remaining milk in a saucepan and heat over medium heat, stirring occasionally, 2 to 3 minutes until the sugar melts. Bring to a boil over high heat, then remove from the heat and pour the mixture over the egg mixture in a thin stream, whisking continuously.

2 Return the mixture to the pan and continue whisking over medium heat 5 to 6 minutes until thickened. Remove from the heat and stir in the vanilla extract and breadcrumbs. Spoon the mixture into an 8-inch round, deep ovenproof dish and set aside.

3 Put the egg whites and salt in a large clean bowl and beat, using an electric mixer, until stiff peaks form. Whisk in the sugar in a thin stream until the meringue is stiff and glossy. Spoon it over the butterscotch and bake 8 to 10 minutes until browned, then serve.

mochamallow mousses

Marshmallows help this egg-free mousse to set very quickly.

2 1/2 cups mini marshmallows
6 tablespoons hot coffee
1/2 cup dark chocolate chips
scant 1 cup heavy cream
1/2 tsp. vanilla extract

Topping
2 tablespoons dark chocolate chips
1/4 cup heavy cream
1 chocolate muffin, cut into cubes
powdered sugar, for dusting
chocolate curls (optional; see page 9), to decorate

1 Put four freezerproof glasses or bowls in the freezer to chill and fill a sink with 2 inches of iced water. Put the marshmallows and coffee in a saucepan and cook over low heat, stirring, 3 to 4 minutes, until melted. Remove from the heat, add the chocolate chips, and stir until melted. Put the pan in the iced water and let cool 2 minutes, stirring.

2 Put the cream and vanilla in a large bowl and beat, using an electric mixer, until it just holds its shape. Add the cooled chocolate and whip 1 to 2 minutes until thick. Spoon the mousse into the chilled glasses and freeze 5 to 10 minutes until set.

3 Meanwhile, put the chocolate chips and cream for the topping in a heatproof bowl and rest it over a pan of gently simmering water, making sure the bottom of the bowl does not touch the water. Heat, stirring occasionally, 2 to 3 minutes until the chocolate melts. Top the mousses with the muffin pieces, then spoon the chocolate sauce over them and dust with powdered sugar. Decorate with chocolate curls, if desired, and serve.

25-minute desserts

chocolate soufflés

These soufflés are rich, delicious, and surprisingly easy to make.

1 Preheat the oven to 400°F with a baking sheet inside. Put the chocolate chips and brandy in a heatproof bowl and rest it over a pan of gently simmering water, making sure the bottom of the bowl does not touch the water. Heat, stirring occasionally, 2 to 3 minutes until the chocolate melts, then remove the bowl from the heat and set aside to cool slightly.

2 Meanwhile, grease four 7-ounce ramekins with melted butter and dust the inside of each one with 1 teaspoon granulated sugar. Stir the egg yolks into the cooled chocolate.

3 Put the egg whites and salt in a clean bowl and beat, using an electric mixer, until stiff peaks form. Whisk in the granulated sugar in a thin stream and continue whisking until the meringue is stiff and glossy. Stir one-quarter of the meringue into the chocolate to lighten it, then fold in the rest. Spoon the mixture into the ramekins and level by scraping a palette knife across the tops, removing any excess mixture. Bake on the baking sheet for 12–13 minutes until well risen. Dust with powdered sugar and serve immediately.

2/3 cup dark chocolate chips
2 tbsp. brandy
melted butter, for greasing
scant 1/3 cup granulated sugar, plus 4 tsp. for dusting
4 eggs, separated
a pinch of salt
powdered sugar, for dusting

ice cream bites (see page 148)

CHAPTER SIX

30-minute desserts

With a full half an hour to devote to dessert, there's no reason why it can't be anything short of magnificent. For a taste of the Middle East, try delicious Baby Baklavas—their crisp layers of phyllo pastry and walnuts drenched in a sweet honey syrup will melt in your mouth. Apricot & Almond Crumble is a classic, comforting choice that's full of juicy fruit covered with a crunchy, nutty topping. And when it comes to perennial favorites, nothing beats hot Chocolate Fondant Puddings—their short baking time creates a molten middle that mingles irresistibly with a cold, creamy accompaniment. These recipes are sure to satisfy everyone's craving for something yummy.

apple & berry charlotte

Bread makes an easy and crisp topping for fruit and a nice alternative to a traditional pie or crumble.

2 apples, peeled, cored,
  and cut into $1/2$in. chunks
$1^1/2$ cups fresh or frozen berries,
  such as raspberries, blueberries,
  and blackberries
$1/3$ cup granulated sugar
3 tbsp. butter, softened
8 slices of slightly stale white
  bread, crusts removed
light cream, to serve

1 Preheat the oven to 400°F with a baking sheet inside. Put the apples and berries in a 4-cup baking dish and mix well. Set aside 1 tablespoon of the granulated sugar and toss the rest with the apples and berries, then set aside.

2 Spread the butter thinly over one side of each slice of bread and cut the slices into triangles. Arrange the triangles over the fruit, buttered-sides up, and sprinkle with the reserved granulated sugar.

3 Bake on the preheated baking sheet 20 to 25 minutes until the bread is crisp and golden and the fruit is soft. Serve hot with cream.

tempura bananas with toffee sauce

A Japanese-inspired batter gives these banana fritters a crisp, light texture.

3 cups canola oil, for deep-frying
$1/2$ cup all-purpose flour
2 tbsp. cornstarch
a pinch of salt
6 tbsp. ice-cold sparkling water
3 large bananas, peeled and each
  cut into 4 chunks
1 tsp. powdered sugar, to serve

TOFFEE SAUCE:
scant $1/2$ cup granulated sugar
$1/4$ cup heavy cream

1 To make the toffee sauce, put the granulated sugar and 2 tablespoons water in a small saucepan and cook over medium heat 1 to 2 minutes, stirring occasionally, until the sugar dissolves. Bring to a boil over high heat and boil 3 to 4 minutes until caramel in color. Remove from the heat and carefully add the cream, stirring to dissolve any lumps, then set aside.

2 Heat the oil in a large deep saucepan or deep-fat fryer to 375°F. Put the flour, cornstarch, and salt in a bowl and stir in the sparkling water, using a fork, to make a thin batter.

3 Working in batches to avoid overcrowding the pan, dip the banana pieces in the batter and carefully put them in the oil. Fry 2 to 3 minutes, turning regularly, until crisp and puffed. Remove from the oil, using a slotted spoon, and drain on paper towel.

4 Just before the fritters are done cooking, warm the toffee sauce over low heat. Serve the bananas dusted with powdered sugar and drizzled with the toffee sauce.

blueberry buckles

These cakes get their name because the fruit and topping tend to cause the cakes to "buckle" rather than rise evenly.

1 Preheat the oven to 400°F and generously butter four cups of a deep nonstick muffin pan. To make the topping, put the melted butter, all-purpose flour, brown sugar, and ginger in a bowl and stir until the mixture looks like large crumbs, then set aside.

2 Put the butter, granulated sugar, egg, self-rising flour, vanilla extract, and salt in another bowl and beat, using an electric mixer, until just combined, then fold in the blueberries. Spoon the batter into the muffin cups and sprinkle with the topping.

3 Bake 20 minutes until risen, golden, and firm to the touch. Turn out the cakes and dust with powdered sugar, then serve warm with whipped cream.

$1/4$ cup ($1/2$ stick) butter, softened, plus melted butter for greasing
$1/4$ cup granulated sugar
1 egg
$1/2$ cup self-rising flour
$1/2$ tsp. vanilla extract
a pinch of salt
$1/3$ cup blueberries
powdered sugar, to decorate
whipped cream, to serve

TOPPING:
1 tbsp. butter, melted
2 tbsp. all-purpose flour
1 tbsp. light brown sugar
$1/4$ tsp. ground ginger

rhubarb crumble

Partially cooking the rhubarb at the beginning of this recipe substantially reduces this crumble's time in the oven.

1 Preheat the oven to 400°F with a baking sheet inside. Put the rhubarb, granulated sugar, and orange zest in a large skillet and cook over medium heat, stirring occasionally, 5 minutes or until the juices start to run and the sugar dissolves.

2 Meanwhile, to make the crumble topping, put the flour, butter, and ginger, if using, in a food processor and blend 1 minute, or until the mixture resembles breadcrumbs. Add the brown sugar and pulse 2 to 3 times to combine.

3 Spoon the rhubarb into a deep 8-inch ovenproof serving dish and sprinkle with the crumble topping. Bake on the preheated baking sheet 20 minutes or until the topping is brown and the filling is bubbling. Serve hot with cream.

1lb. 4oz. rhubarb, cut into $1/2$in. pieces
$1/3$ cup granulated sugar
finely grated zest of 1 large orange

CRUMBLE TOPPING:
$1 1/2$ cups all-purpose flour
3 tbsp. butter, cut into large cubes
1 tsp. ground ginger (optional)
$1/3$ cup packed light brown sugar
light cream or vanilla ice cream, to serve

plum & walnut torte

Ground walnuts give this cake a wonderful taste and texture.

1/2 cup (1 stick) butter, softened,
  plus extra for greasing
1lb. 8oz. red plums, halved, pitted,
  and each half halved again
3/4 cup plus 2 tbsp. granulated
  sugar
scant 1/2 cup chopped walnuts
2 eggs
1/2 tsp. vanilla extract
3/4 cup plus 2 tbsp. self-rising flour
powdered sugar, to decorate

1 Preheat the oven to 400°F. Grease an 8-inch round cake pan with butter and line the bottom with baking parchment cut to fit. Put the plums in two baking dishes, cut-sides up, and sprinkle with 1/3 cup of the granulated sugar.

2 Put the walnuts in a food processor and blend until finely ground. Add the butter, eggs, vanilla extract, flour, and remaining granulated sugar and pulse until just combined. Scrape the mixture into the cake pan and smooth the surface. Put the plums on the lower shelf of the oven and the cake on the middle shelf. Bake 20 minutes or until the plums are slightly softened and the cake is brown and firm to the touch. Remove the cake and plums from the oven and let cool 2 to 3 minutes.

3 Carefully turn the cake out onto a plate. Peel off the parchment and arrange the plums on top. Dust the cake with powdered sugar and serve.

dutch apple pancake

This pancake is baked in the oven rather than fried, so it's puffy and light.

1/4 cup (1/2 stick) butter
2 large crisp apples, such
  as Granny Smith, peeled,
  quartered, cored and each
  quarter sliced into 3 pieces
1/4 cup packed light brown sugar
1 tsp. ground ginger
3 eggs
2/3 cup all-purpose flour
1/2 cup milk
a pinch of salt
powdered sugar, to decorate
light cream, to serve

1 Preheat the oven to 450°F. Melt the butter in a large heavy-bottomed, ovenproof skillet over medium heat. When it is foaming, add the apples, brown sugar, and ginger and cook, stirring occasionally, 5 minutes until the sugar dissolves and the apples have softened slightly.

2 Meanwhile, put the eggs, flour, milk, and salt in a blender and blend 1 to 2 minutes until smooth. Pour the batter into the pan and immediately transfer it to the oven. Bake 10 minutes, then lower the oven temperature to 400°F and bake another 10 minutes until puffed up and golden.

3 Remove from the oven and dust with powdered sugar. Cut and serve the pancake from the pan and drizzle with cream.

apricot & almond crumble

Crumbles can take a long time to bake, but using a very soft fruit, such as apricots, speeds up the time considerably.

1 Preheat the oven to 400°F with a baking sheet inside. Put the apricots in an 8-inch ovenproof serving dish and sprinkle with 2 tablespoons of the granulated sugar, then set aside.

2 Put the almonds in a food processor and blend until coarsely chopped. Add the flour and butter and blend again until the mixture resembles breadcrumbs. Add the remaining granulated sugar and pulse to combine, then sprinkle the mixture over the apricots.

3 Bake on the preheated baking sheet 20 to 25 minutes until the filling is bubbling and the topping is crisp and golden brown. Spoon into four bowls and serve hot with ice cream.

2lb. apricots, halved, pitted, and
  each half halved again
scant $1/2$ cup granulated sugar
$1/3$ cup blanched almonds
scant 1 cup all-purpose flour
3 tbsp. cold butter
vanilla ice cream or light cream,
  to serve

banana tarte tatins

Bananas cook quickly and make an interesting, unexpected topping for a tarte tatin, replacing the more usual apples.

1 Preheat the oven to 425°F and line a baking sheet with foil. Grease four 3-inch loose-bottomed tart pans with melted butter and line the bottoms with baking parchment circles cut to fit. Sprinkle the granulated sugar over the bottoms of the pans.

2 Put the bananas in the pans, cut-sides up, trimming to fit as necessary. Cut out four rounds from the puff pastry, using a $3^1/2$-inch cookie cutter, and cover the bananas, tucking the edges of the pastry into the pans. Put the pans on the baking sheet and bake 13 to 14 minutes until the pastry is risen, golden, and crisp.

3 Remove the baking sheet from the oven and cover with a large cutting board. Using oven mitts or folded dish towels, carefully invert the baking sheet to drop the tarts onto the cutting board. Peel away the foil and carefully lift off the pans, bottoms, and baking parchment, repositioning any loose pieces of banana with the tip of a knife. Transfer the tarts to four plates and serve with cream.

melted butter, for greasing
2 tbsp. granulated sugar
3 slightly underripe bananas,
  peeled and halved lengthwise
1 sheet of ready-rolled puff
  pastry, about 9oz.
light cream, to serve

spiced caramel kumquat compote

Kumquats, with their sweet rind and tart fruit, make a colorful winter compote.

1½ cups granulated sugar
1lb. kumquats, each sliced into
   4 pieces crosswise
2 star anise
2 small cinnamon sticks
5 whole black peppercorns
2 cups vanilla ice cream

1 Put the sugar and 4 tablespoons water in a saucepan and cook, stirring, over medium heat 2 to 3 minutes until the sugar dissolves. Bring to a boil over high heat and boil 4 to 5 minutes, swirling the pan occasionally, until the sugar turns a caramel color.

2 Remove from the heat and carefully add scant ⅔ cup water. Protect your hand, as the caramel may splutter.

3 Return the caramel to a low heat and add the kumquats, star anise, cinnamon, and peppercorns. Cook, stirring, until any traces of hard caramel have dissolved.

4 Bring to a boil again, then reduce the heat to low and simmer 15 minutes until the kumquats are tender. Shortly before serving, remove the ice cream from the freezer and let stand at room temperature to soften slightly. Serve the warm kumquat over the ice cream.

rustic apple pie

Free-formed fruit pies are quick to make and have a rustic charm that's welcomed at the end of a meal.

1 sheet of rolled pie crust,
   about 8oz.
2 large apples, peeled, cored,
   and sliced
2 tbsp. granulated sugar
¼ tsp. cinnamon (optional)
1 egg, beaten
powdered sugar, to serve
ice cream or whipped cream,
   to serve

1 Preheat the oven to 400°F and line a baking sheet with baking parchment. Cut out a rough 11-inch round from the pastry and put it on the baking sheet.

2 Put the apples on the pastry, heaping them up slightly towards the center and leaving a 1½-inch-wide border of pastry around the edge. Sprinkle with the granulated sugar and cinnamon, if using. Bring the border of the pastry inwards over the apples, pleating and folding as you go so it lies flat over the edge of the apples. Brush the pastry with the egg.

3 Bake 20 minutes or until the pastry is golden brown and the apples have softened slightly. Dust with powdered sugar and serve hot with ice cream.

ginger & apricot baked apples

Cutting the apples in half speeds up their time in the oven, so dessert gets to the table faster.

1 Preheat the oven to 400°F and grease a baking dish large enough to hold the apple halves upright with butter. Put the apples in the dish, cut-sides up. Put the apricots, sugar, and preserved and ground ginger in a small bowl and mix well, then pack this mixture into the center of the apple halves, where the cores used to be. Divide the butter over the tops of the apple halves.

2 Fill the dish 1/4-inch deep with water and bake 10 minutes, then baste by spooning the juices in the dish over the apples.

3 Bake another 15 minutes or until the apples are soft. Check occasionally and add a splash of water if the dish becomes too dry. Carefully transfer the apples to bowls and spoon any juices from the baking dish over the top. Serve hot with cream.

2 tbsp. butter, cut into 4 pieces, plus extra for greasing
4 floury-type apples, such as Spartan or Macintosh, halved crosswise and cored
8 dried apricots, chopped
2 tbsp. light brown sugar
2 tsp. chopped candied ginger
1/4 tsp. ground ginger
light cream, to serve

sticky toffee puddings

Baking individual puddings makes this dessert elegant enough to be served at even the most stylish dinner parties.

1 Preheat the oven to 400°F and generously butter four 7-ounce molds or ramekins. Put half of the butter in a bowl and add the granulated sugar, flour, egg, vanilla extract, and salt. Beat, using an electric mixer, until just combined, then stir in the dates and walnuts. Spoon the mixture into the molds and bake 20 to 22 minutes until risen, golden, and firm.

2 Shortly before the puddings are done baking, put the brown sugar, cream, and remaining butter in a saucepan and cook over low heat, stirring continuously, until the sugar dissolves. Bring to a boil and cook over high heat, stirring, 1 minute, then set aside.

3 Carefully unmold each pudding onto a plate, right-side up. Spoon the warm sauce over the puddings and serve with extra cream for pouring over.

1/2 cup (1 stick) butter, softened, plus extra for greasing
1/4 cup granulated sugar
1/2 cup self-rising flour
1 egg
1/2 tsp. vanilla extract
a pinch of salt
4 pitted dates, coarsely chopped
2 tbsp. chopped walnuts
1/2 cup packed light brown sugar
scant 1/2 cup heavy cream, plus extra for serving

peach galette

A puff-pastry tart shell makes an impressive container for sweet summer peaches.

1 sheet of ready-rolled puff
   pastry, about 9oz.
2 large peaches, halved, pitted,
   and very thinly sliced
1 tbsp. vanilla sugar (see page 40)
   or granulated sugar
1 egg, beaten
2 tbsp. apricot jam
whipped cream or vanilla ice
   cream, to serve

1 Preheat the oven to 425°F and line a large baking sheet with baking parchment. Put the pastry on the baking sheet and mark a $1/2$-inch-wide border all round it, using a sharp knife, then prick inside the border, using a fork. Spread the peach slices over the pastry, keeping them inside the border. Sprinkle the sugar over the peaches, then brush the border of the pastry with the egg.

2 Bake 15 minutes or until the pastry is golden underneath and puffed at the edges. Meanwhile, put the jam in a small saucepan and heat over low heat, stirring, 1 to 2 minutes until runny.

3 Remove the galette from the oven and slide it onto a serving plate. Brush the peaches with the warm jam, then slice and serve with whipped cream.

lemon surprise puddings

The surprise when you dig into these puddings is a zesty lemon curd on the bottom.

2 tbsp. butter, softened, plus
   extra for greasing
1 egg, separated, plus 1 egg white
a large pinch of salt
scant $1/2$ cup granulated sugar
juice and finely grated zest
   of 1 lemon
2 tbsp. milk
$1/2$ cup all-purpose flour
light cream, to serve

1 Preheat the oven to 400°F and bring a kettle of water to a boil. Grease four 7-ounce ramekins with butter and put them in a small roasting pan. Put the egg whites and salt in a large clean bowl and beat, using an electric mixer, until stiff peaks form, then set aside.

2 In a separate bowl, use the mixer (no need to wash the beaters) to beat together the egg yolk, butter, granulated sugar, lemon juice and zest, milk, and flour until just combined (it may look a little curdled). Stir in one-quarter of the egg whites to loosen, then fold in the remaining egg whites. Spoon the batter into the ramekins.

3 Put the ramekins in the pan and add enough boiling water to the pan to come half-way up the sides of the ramekins. Bake 17 to 20 minutes or until risen and just firm to the touch. Serve hot with cream.

apple spice cakes

Warm, dense apple cake is a delicious autumnal dessert, and these muffin-sized ones make delightful individual treats.

scant 1 cup self-rising flour
$1/4$ tsp. baking soda
1 tsp. pumpkin pie spice
$1/2$ tsp. ground ginger
a large pinch of salt
$1/2$ cup (1 stick) butter, softened
$1/2$ cup packed light brown sugar
2 eggs
$1/2$ tsp. vanilla extract
1 tbsp. plain yogurt
1 apple, grated
$2/3$ cup raisins
1 tbsp. demerara sugar
vanilla ice cream or whipped cream,
  to serve

1 Preheat the oven to 375°F and line 8 cups of a muffin pan with paper cupcake liners. Sift the flour, baking soda, pumpkin pie spice, ginger, and salt into a large bowl. Add the butter, brown sugar, eggs, vanilla extract, and yogurt and beat, using an electric mixer, until just combined. Fold in the apple and raisins.

2 Spoon the batter into the cupcake liners and sprinkle with the demerara sugar. Bake 20 minutes or until firm to the touch.

3 Carefully remove the cakes from the pan and set aside to cool 1 to 2 minutes, then peel the papers off. Serve with ice cream.

pear & almond puddings

Bursting with ripe fruit and nutty almonds, this puddings makes a wonderful, comforting dessert.

$1/4$ cup ($1/2$ stick) butter, softened,
  plus extra for greasing
2 large, ripe pears, peeled,
  quartered and cored, then each
  quarter quartered again
$1/3$ cup granulated sugar
1 egg
$1/4$ cup self-rising flour
$1/4$ cup ground almonds
3 drops of almond extract
1 tbsp. slivered almonds (optional)
light cream or vanilla ice cream,
  to serve

1 Preheat the oven to 400°F and grease four 7-ounce ramekins with butter. Put the pears in the ramekins and sprinkle each one with 1 tablespoon of the granulated sugar.

2 Put the butter, egg, flour, almonds, almond extract, and remaining granulated sugar in a large bowl and beat, using an electric mixer, until just combined. Spoon the batter over the pears, then sprinkle with the slivered almonds, if using.

3 Put the ramekins on a baking sheet and bake 20 minutes, or until the cake is risen, golden, and firm to the touch. Serve hot with cream.

raspberry sponge drops

Made with a sponge cake mixture but dropped free-form onto baking sheets, these can be stacked to make pretty towers layered with cream and berries.

1 Preheat the oven to 350°F and line two baking sheets with baking parchment. Put the butter, granulated sugar, flour, egg, vanilla extract, and salt in a bowl and beat, using an electric mixer, 2 to 3 minutes until just combined.

2 Drop 12 tablespoonfuls of the mixture onto the baking sheets, spacing well apart. Bake 10 to 12 minutes until golden and firm to the touch. Carefully slide the parchment and sponge drops onto wire racks and let cool 5 minutes.

3 Meanwhile, put the cream and powdered sugar in a bowl and beat, using an electric mixer, until stiff peaks form. Put 1 sponge drop on each of four plates and divide half the whipped cream over them. Nestle half of the raspberries into the cream and then layer again. Top with the remaining sponge drops and serve dusted with powdered sugar.

$^1/_4$ cup ($^1/_2$ stick) butter, softened
$^1/_4$ cup granulated sugar
$^1/_2$ cup self-rising flour
1 egg
$^1/_4$ tsp. vanilla extract
a pinch of salt
1 cup heavy cream
1 tsp. powdered sugar, plus extra to serve
$1^1/_2$ cups raspberries

blueberry "pie"

Blueberries are a perfect summer pie filling, and using frozen ones means you can enjoy this all-American treat all year round.

1 Preheat the oven to 425°F with a baking sheet inside. Put the blueberries and cornstarch in a bowl and toss well. Set aside 1 tablespoon of the granulated sugar and stir the rest into the blueberries. Put the blueberries in an 8-inch pie plate and brush the edge of the dish with a little of the egg.

2 Lay the pastry over the dish and press onto the edge of the pie plate to secure. Trim away any excess pastry, using a sharp knife, then press the edges of the crust with a fork to seal. Brush the crust with the egg, sprinkle with the remaining granulated sugar, and cut a small steam hole in the center.

3 Bake on the preheated baking sheet 20 minutes or until the crust is golden brown. Serve hot with ice cream.

1lb. fresh or frozen blueberries (about 3 cups)
2 tbsp. cornstarch
$1/3$ cup granulated sugar
1 egg, beaten
1 sheet of rolled pie crust, about 8oz.
vanilla ice cream or whipped cream, to serve

hot chocolate, raisin & rum pudding

The liquid poured over the top of this pudding transforms during baking into a rich sauce sitting under chocolate cake.

1 Preheat the oven to 400°F with a baking sheet inside and grease a deep 8-inch ovenproof serving dish with oil. Put the brown sugar, rum, 2 tablespoons of the cocoa powder, and scant $2/3$ cup water in a small saucepan and heat over medium heat 2 to 3 minutes, whisking occasionally, until the sugar dissolves.

2 Meanwhile, put the chocolate chips, flour, granulated sugar, and remaining cocoa powder in a food processor and blend 1 minute until the chocolate is finely chopped. Add the egg, oil, and milk and blend 1 minute until well mixed, then add the raisins and pulse 1 or 2 times to combine.

3 Pour the chocolate mixture into the dish, then spoon the rum mixture over the top. Bake on the preheated baking sheet 20 minutes or until risen and firm to the touch and a sauce has formed underneath the sponge cake. Serve hot with cream.

3 tbsp. sunflower oil, plus extra for greasing
$1/2$ cup packed light brown sugar
$1/4$ cup dark rum
$1/3$ cup cocoa powder
scant $2/3$ cup dark chocolate chips
scant $12/3$ cups self-rising flour
1 cup granulated sugar
1 egg
$3/4$ cup milk
$1/4$ cup raisins
light cream, to serve

▶ice cream bites

Small bites of chocolate and ice cream are a great way to finish a meal. These can be served as dessert, or with coffee if you're really in a hurry and want to skip the dessert course.

1¼ cups dark chocolate chips
1 cup strawberry ice cream
2 small strawberries, thinly sliced,
  to decorate

1 Put the chocolate chips in a heatproof bowl and rest it over a pan of gently simmering water, making sure the bottom of the bowl does not touch the water. Heat, stirring occasionally, 2 to 3 minutes, until the chocolate melts. Remove the bowl from the heat and set aside to cool slightly.

2 Meanwhile, line a mini muffin pan that will fit in your freezer with 8 mini paper cupcake liners. Spoon some of the chocolate into the bottom of each one and spread it up the sides of the liner, using the back of a teaspoon. Freeze 5 minutes or until the chocolate has become firm, then apply a second layer of chocolate and return to the freezer another 5 minutes or until firm. Meanwhile, remove the ice cream from the freezer and let stand at room temperature to soften slightly.

3 Remove the paper liners from the pan and gently peel the paper away. If necessary, warm the outside of the cups slightly with your hands to help the paper peel away. Using a melon baller, scoop 1 small ball of ice cream into each of the chocolate cups, decorate with a slice of strawberry, and serve immediately.

sticky sponge pudding

This classic British dessert comes together so easily, and is so yummy, it's no wonder it's been popular for such a long time.

½ cup (1 stick) butter, softened,
  plus extra for greasing
scant 1 cup light corn syrup or
  golden syrup
½ cup granulated sugar
scant 1 cup self-rising flour
1 egg, beaten
½ tsp. vanilla extract
½ tsp. ground ginger
a pinch of salt
light cream, to serve

1 Preheat the oven to 400°F and generously grease an 8-inch ovenproof serving dish with butter. Pour half of the corn syrup into the dish and set aside.

2 Put the butter and granulated sugar in a large bowl and beat, using an electric mixer, 1 to 2 minutes until fluffy. Add the flour, egg, vanilla extract, ginger, and salt and beat until just combined. Spoon the mixture into the dish and bake 20 to 25 minutes until the sponge cake is risen, golden, and just firm to the touch.

3 Meanwhile, warm the remaining corn syrup in a small pan over a low heat. Serve the sponge with the extra syrup and cream.

baby baklavas

Baklava can be complicated to make, so try this easy version instead, which looks as good as it tastes.

3 tbsp. butter, melted, plus extra
  for greasing
4 sheets of phyllo pastry
1/2 cup walnuts, finely chopped
scant 1/2 cup honey
Greek yogurt, to serve
2 tablespoons chopped pistachios

1 Preheat the oven to 400°F and grease a large baking sheet with some of the melted butter. Put 1 sheet of phyllo pastry on the baking sheet and keep the rest covered with a clean, damp dish towel while you work. Brush with butter, trim any overhanging pastry, then repeat with a second layer of phyllo. Sprinkle half of the walnuts over the pasty and cover with the remaining sheets of phyllo, brushing with butter between each layer and trimming any overhanging pastry. Bake 8 to 10 minutes, until golden and crisp. Meanwhile, warm the honey and 2 tablespoons water in a small saucepan over low heat.

2 Slide the baklava onto a cutting board and let cool 2 minutes, then cut the baklava into 8 rectangles, using a large, sharp knife. Cut each rectangle in half diagonally to make triangles and stack them on a serving plate, drizzling a little of the honey syrup between each layer. Sprinkle with the pistachios, then serve with yogurt and any remaining honey sauce.

easy carrot halwa

This rich, simple version of the popular Indian dessert is delicious served warm with ice cream.

1 Put the carrots, both milks, brown sugar, and ginger in a large skillet or wok and cook over medium heat, stirring, 2 to 3 minutes until the sugar dissolves. Bring to a boil over high heat and boil, uncovered, 10 minutes, stirring occasionally.
2 Add the butter, reduce the heat to low, and simmer, uncovered, another 10 minutes or until the liquid has been absorbed and the carrot has turned a deep golden color.
3 Remove from the heat and stir in the raisins, almonds, and pistachios. Let stand 5 minutes, then spoon the halwa into four bowls and serve with ice cream.

1lb. carrots, peeled and coarsely grated
14fl. oz. canned sweetened condensed milk
$1/2$ cup whole milk
$1/4$ cup packed light brown sugar
$1/2$ tsp. ground ginger
2 tbsp. butter
$1/4$ cup raisins
$1/4$ cup slivered almonds
$1/4$ cup unsalted pistachios, chopped
vanilla ice cream, to serve

ginger puddings with white chocolate sauce

Sticky, spicy ginger puddings with a vanilla-scented sauce make a comforting dessert for a cold winter's evening.

1 Preheat the oven to 400°F and generously butter four 7-ounce ramekins or molds. Put the butter, brown sugar, and molasses in a small saucepan and cook over medium heat, stirring, 2 to 3 minutes until the sugar dissolves and the butter melts. Remove from the heat, add the milk, flour, ground ginger, baking soda, and 1 egg yolk, and whisk until smooth.
2 Divide the batter into the ramekins; they will be about half full. Bake 20 minutes or until the cakes are firm on top and shrinking away from the side of the ramekins. Let cool 5 minutes, then unmold onto four plates and sprinkle with the chopped ginger.
3 Meanwhile, put the remaining egg yolk, cornstarch, granulated sugar, and cream in a small saucepan and cook over low heat, whisking continuously, 5 minutes until smooth and thickened. Remove from the heat, add the chocolate chips, and stir until melted. Serve the puddings with the sauce.

$1/4$ cup ($1/2$ stick) butter, softened, plus extra for greasing
$1/4$ cup packed light brown sugar
3 tbsp. molasses
$1/3$ cup milk
$1/3$ cup all-purpose flour
1 tsp. ground ginger
$1/2$ tsp. baking soda
2 egg yolks
1 tsp. chopped candied ginger
$1 1/2$ tsp. cornstarch
$1 1/2$ tsp. granulated sugar
$2/3$ cup heavy cream
$1/4$ cup white chocolate chips

chocolate croissant puddings

This is a clever way to turn a breakfast favorite into an outstanding dessert.

2 chocolate croissants, torn into
  bite-size pieces
scant 1 cup milk
scant 1 cup heavy cream
2 egg yolks
2 tbsp. granulated sugar
1 tbsp. cornstarch
1/4 tsp. vanilla extract
powdered sugar, to serve

1 Preheat the oven to 350°F and bring a kettle of water to a boil. Divide the croissant pieces into four 7-ounce ramekins and put the ramekins in a small roasting pan. Put the milk and cream in a large saucepan and bring just to boiling over medium heat, then set aside.

2 Put the egg yolks, granulated sugar, cornstarch, and vanilla extract in a bowl and whisk together, then whisk in the hot milk mixture in a thin stream. Return the mixture to the saucepan and cook over medium heat, whisking continuously, 2 to 3 minutes until slightly thickened. Pour the custard into the ramekins.

3 Pour enough boiling water into the roasting pan to come half way up the sides of the ramekins. Bake 20 minutes or until the custard has just set. Remove the ramekins from the water, dust the tops with a little powdered sugar, and serve hot.

▶ chocolate fondant puddings

These classic chocolate puddings have irresistible melting centers.

1/2 cup (1 stick) butter, plus extra
  for greasing
scant 2/3 cup dark chocolate chips
2 eggs, plus 2 egg yolks
1/4 cup granulated sugar
1/2 tsp. vanilla extract
a pinch of salt
2 tbsp. all-purpose flour
1 tbsp. cocoa powder
vanilla ice cream, to serve
raspberries, to serve

1 Preheat the oven to 375°F and generously grease four 7-ounce ramekins or molds with butter. Put the chocolate chips and butter in a heatproof bowl and rest it over a pan of gently simmering water, making sure the bottom of the bowl does not touch the water. Heat, stirring occasionally, 4 to 5 minutes until melted. Remove the bowl from the heat.

2 Put the eggs, egg yolks, granulated sugar, vanilla extract, and salt in a large bowl and beat, using an electric mixer, 4 to 5 minutes until the mixture is pale, mousse-like, and three times its original volume. Drizzle the chocolate mixture into the bowl and sift in the flour and cocoa, then fold together until just combined.

3 Spoon the mixture into the molds and put them on a baking sheet. Bake 10 minutes or until just set on top. Remove from the oven and let stand 1 minute, then turn them out onto four plates and serve immediately with ice cream and berries.

peanut butter pie

Peanut butter pie is an American diner classic that will satisfy anyone with a sweet tooth.

7oz. graham crackers
6 tbsp. (³/₄ stick) butter
²/₃ cup dark chocolate chips
8oz. (1 cup) cream cheese
1 cup smooth peanut butter
¹/₂ cup powdered sugar
¹/₂ cup heavy cream
1 large banana, peeled and sliced, to serve
1oz. milk chocolate, to decorate

1 Put the graham crackers in a plastic bag and crush to fine crumbs, using a rolling pin, then set aside. Melt the butter and chocolate chips in a small saucepan over very low heat, stirring occasionally. Add the crumbs and stir until well coated in the chocolate mixture. Press the crumbs firmly into the bottom of an 8-inch loose-bottomed tart pan and freeze 5 minutes.

2 Meanwhile, put the cream cheese, peanut butter, and powdered sugar in a bowl and beat, using an electric mixer, 1 to 2 minutes until smooth. Add the cream and beat again until combined.

3 Spoon the filling into the crumb base and return the pie to the freezer another 15 minutes.

4 Carefully remove the outer ring of the tart pan and transfer the pie to a serving plate. Peel and slice the banana and arrange the pieces around the edge, then grate the chocolate over the pie. Serve immediately.

chocolate-mint mousses

Traditional dark chocolate mousse is spiked with refreshing mint.

²/₃ cup dark chocolate chips
4 eggs, separated
¹/₄ tsp. peppermint extract
2 tbsp. granulated sugar
chocolate-coated mint wafers, to decorate
mint sprigs, to decorate

1 Put four freezerproof glasses or bowls in the freezer to chill. Put the chocolate chips in a large heatproof bowl and rest it over a pan of gently simmering water, making sure the bottom of the bowl does not touch the water. Heat, stirring occasionally, 2 to 3 minutes until the chocolate melts. Remove the bowl from the heat and set aside to cool slightly.

2 Beat the egg yolks and peppermint extract together, then stir this mixture into the chocolate and set aside. Put the egg whites in a clean bowl and beat, using an electric mixer, until stiff peaks form. Whisk in the granulated sugar in a thin stream and continue whisking until the meringue is stiff and glossy.

3 Stir one-quarter of the meringue into the chocolate mixture to lighten, then fold in the rest. Spoon the mousse into the chilled glasses and return to the freezer 10 minutes. Serve decorated with chocolate-coated mint wafers and mint sprigs.

cinnamon-sugared churros

Spaniards love these light doughnuts for breakfast, but they are just as delicious served for dessert.

1 Heat the oil in a deep heavy-bottomed saucepan or deep-fat fryer to 350°F. Preheat the oven to 150°F. Put the butter, salt, and 1 cup water in a saucepan and heat over medium heat, stirring, until the butter melts. Bring to a boil and boil 1 minute. Remove from the heat, add the flour, and beat with a wooden spoon until a ball of dough forms. Transfer the dough to a bowl and let cool 5 minutes.
2 Beat the eggs into the dough, one at a time, with the wooden spoon, until a thick mixture forms. Spoon the mixture into a pastry bag fitted with a $1/2$-inch star nozzle. Mix the powdered sugar and cinnamon together in a bowl and set aside.
3 Working in batches to avoid overcrowding the pan, squeeze 4-inch strips of batter into the hot oil and fry 4 minutes, turning regularly, until golden. Remove from the oil, using a slotted spoon, and drain on paper towel. Keep warm in the oven while you fry the rest. Dust with the cinnamon sugar and serve hot.

3 cups canola oil, for deep-frying
$1/2$ cup (1 stick) butter, diced
$1/4$ tsp. salt
scant 1 cup all-purpose flour
3 eggs
2 tbsp. powdered sugar
$1/4$ tsp. cinnamon

thai forbidden rice pudding

The black "forbidden" rice in this Thai favorite turns a deep purple color when cooked, making a stunning presentation.

1 Put the rice, vanilla bean, coconut milk, and milk in a large heavy-bottomed saucepan and bring to a boil over high heat. Reduce the heat to medium and simmer 25 minutes, stirring occasionally and adding extra milk, if needed.
2 Meanwhile, put the sesame seeds in a dry skillet and cook over medium heat, stirring frequently, 2 to 3 minutes until golden and fragrant. Immediately transfer to a plate to cool.
3 Remove the vanilla bean from the rice and scrape the seeds out into the rice. Add the granulated sugar and stir well, then divide the rice into bowls. Top with whipped cream and sprinkle with the sesame seeds. Serve hot with extra sugar for stirring in, if desired.

1 heaping cup black forbidden rice
1 vanilla bean, halved
$13/4$ cups coconut milk
$11/4$ cups milk, plus extra if needed
1 tbsp. sesame seeds
2 tbsp. granulated sugar, plus extra (optional) to serve
whipped cream, to serve

▶ warm chocolate roulade

This chocolate roulade, made with a thin sponge cake, bakes quickly—so it can be on the table faster than you might imagine.

3 eggs, at room temperature
1/2 tsp. vanilla extract
scant 1/2 cup granulated sugar
1/3 cup cocoa powder
scant 1/2 cup all-purpose flour
6 tbsp. raspberry jam
1 tbsp. powdered sugar, for dusting
raspberries, to serve
whipped cream (optional), to serve

1 Preheat the oven to 350°F and line a 13 x 9-inch jelly roll pan with baking parchment, leaving some parchment hanging over the edges of the pan. Put the eggs and vanilla extract in a large bowl. Set aside 1 tablespoon of the granulated sugar and add the rest to the eggs. Beat, using an electric mixer, 4 to 5 minutes until the mixture is pale, mousse-like and about four times its original volume.

2 Sift the cocoa and flour into the egg mixture and fold in. Spoon the batter into the jelly roll pan and gently level the surface. Bake 10 to 12 minutes until risen and firm to the touch.

3 Meanwhile, put a large piece of baking parchment on a work surface and sprinkle it with the reserved granulated sugar. Put the jam in a small saucepan and heat over low heat, stirring, 1 to 2 minutes until runny. Turn out the cake onto the parchment, spread the jam over it, and gently roll up from one of the short ends, using the parchment as a guide. Dust with powdered sugar, then slice. Serve with raspberries and whipped cream, if desired.

ricotta beignets

Ricotta makes these fritters as light as a cloud.

2 cups canola oil, for deep-frying
1/4 cup honey
1 1/4 cups ricotta cheese
2 eggs
2 tbsp. granulated sugar
1 tsp. vanilla extract
2/3 cup self-rising flour
powdered sugar, to serve

1 Heat the oil in a large heavy-bottomed saucepan or deep-fat fryer to 350°F and line a plate with several layers of paper towel. Put the honey and 1 tablespoon water in a small saucepan and cook over low heat, stirring, until bubbling, then set aside.

2 Put the ricotta in a large bowl and beat in the eggs, granulated sugar, and vanilla extract, using an electric mixer, then fold in the flour. Working in batches, drop 3 rounded tablespoons of the batter into the hot oil and fry 2 to 3 minutes, turning often, until golden brown and slightly puffed. Remove from the oil, using a slotted spoon, and drain on paper towel.

3 Dust the beignets with powdered sugar and drizzle with the honey. Serve immediately.

index

index